Praise for *Looking*

"In a world of conflicting identities, Botrus Mansour reflects as an Arab-Palestinian Christian Israeli citizen living in Nazareth. This book comes from a genuine ambassador of reconciliation, encouraging not only individual reflection but motivating meaningful dialogue within the family and among friends, even unlikely ones."
—*Dr. Nina Balmaceda*,
Associate Teaching Professor of the Practice of Reconciliation, Duke Divinity School

"My dear friend and brother Botrus offers deep and rich insights into the scriptures. This is a fresh and thought-provoking perspective on the life of Jesus of Nazareth."
—*Rev. Ray Bentley*, Senior Pastor of Maranatha Chapel, San Diego, California

"As a lawyer, Mansour's legal mind is brought to bear on the challenges that both the church and the community has struggled within this context. He raises your sight and energizes you to think afresh; it is a must-read."
—*Godfrey Yogarajah*, Deputy Secretary-General, World Evangelical Alliance

"Simply fascinating. Very few people have such an amazing 'front-row seat' of one of the most complex cultures on the planet. Enjoy the journey and get ready to evaluate your own heart as you travel down life's road with a trusted guide."
—*Dr. Danny Sinquefield*, Senior Pastor, Faith Baptist Church, Bartlett, Tennessee; past President of the Tennessee Baptist Convention

"It is my privilege to recommend this book of wise reflections and insightful commentary."
—*Dr. Gary Cook*, Chancellor, Dallas Baptist University

"Mansour does not only write from a complex context, but skillfully weaves together biblical concepts with contemporary practical issues that the global church is facing. This is an authentic voice out of Nazareth."
—*Rev. Riad Kassis*, PhD,
International Director, Langham Scholars Ministry, Langham Partnership

"Botrus Mansour does not shy away from difficult questions but urges us to find faithful ways to live together, to combat religious and political fundamentalism, foster peace, justice, and reconciliation. I recommend this book for anyone who wants to learn from a present-day Christian of Nazareth who follows in the footsteps of the Nazarene today —and how that might inform our own walks of faith."

—*Bishop Dr. Munib Younan,*
Honorary President of Religions for Peace, Jerusalem

"Mansour's unique insights help break down barriers and remind people not only of the Good News of the Gospel, but also how the realities of the Christian faith give us hope in the midst of oppression, injustice, and brokenness in this world."

—*Rev. Dr. Mae Elise Cannon,* Executive Director,
Churches for Middle East Peace (CMEP)

"Political and spiritual, challenging and warming, insightful and revealing, all delivered from a delightful Middle Eastern, Palestinian, Christian perspective."

—*David Kerrigan,*
Former General Director, Baptist Mission Society World Mission, UK

"Mansour's witty and thought-provoking book is a must-read for anyone who would like to learn more about Israel, but especially the Palestinian Christians who are a vital part of the Holy Land."

—*Brent McBurney,* President and CEO, Advocates International

"I have known Botrus for five years and have found him to be a man of great faith, intellect, and wisdom. His new book gives an insight into the Arab culture and beyond. It dives deep into topics such as racism, politics, love, faith, church, and community. I highly recommend it to you."

—*Rev. Dr. Jeff Moes,* Senior Pastor, Sunnybrook Church, Sioux City, Iowa

"Mansour writes for Christians who want to be global citizens."

—*Rev. Dr. Jack Sara,* President, Bethlehem Bible College

LOOKING

FROM THE

PRECIPICE

Botrus Mansour

PARACLETE PRESS
BREWSTER, MASSACHUSETTS

To my dear beloved wife A'bir and our children
Atallah, Lamma, and Mai for their encouragement and
support that motivated me to write.

2021 First Printing
Looking from the Precipice: Reflections from Nazareth of a Palestinian Christian Evangelical
Copyright © 2021 by Botrus Mansour
ISBN 978-1-64060-655-5

Library of Congress Cataloging-in-Publication Data
Names: Mansour, Botrus, author.
Title: Looking from the precipice : reflections from Nazareth of a
   Palestinian Christian Evangelical / Botrus Mansour.
Description: Brewster, Massachusetts : Paraclete Press, 2021. | Summary:
   "Urging his readers to turn their hearts towards God and each other,
   this book ranges deeply into Christian devotion, discipleship, mission,
   and current event"-- Provided by publisher.
Identifiers: LCCN 2020042087 (print) | LCCN 2020042088 (ebook) | ISBN
   9781640606555 (trade paperback) | ISBN 9781640606562 (epub) | ISBN
   9781640606579 (pdf)
Subjects: LCSH: Meditations.
Classification: LCC BV4832.3 .M336 2021 (print) | LCC BV4832.3 (ebook) |
   DDC 242--dc23
LC record available at https://lccn.loc.gov/2020042087
LC ebook record available at https://lccn.loc.gov/2020042088

10 9 8 7 6 5 4 3 2 1

Published by Paraclete Press | Brewster, Massachusetts | www.paracletepress.com
Printed in the United States of America

CONTENTS

Part Three *Challenges to Faith*

Part Four *The Work of Church*

A New and Ancient Work

Nazareth is one of those rare places famous for something that did not happen. For generations, Christians have persisted in viewing Nazareth as a place of unbelief and skepticism about its most famous citizen.

Early on in his public ministry of healings and other miracles, Jesus of Nazareth returned to his hometown. But, according to Gospel accounts, he could do no great work there because of the disbelief of its residents.

"And Jesus said to them, 'A prophet is not without honor, except in his hometown and among his relatives and in his own household.' And he could do no mighty work there, except that he laid his hands on a few sick people and healed them. And he marveled because of their unbelief. And he went about among the villages teaching" (Mark 6:4–6, ESV).

A major town in the Roman era, from Jesus's childhood years Nazareth knew him and his family, and it was beyond the imagination of its Jewish elites to consider the possibility that this controversial person could be the long-awaited Messiah. The great story of our redemption through Christ unfolds from the get-go within one family about to be formed in Nazareth. After the birth of Jesus in Bethlehem and the Holy Family's flight into Egypt, this same family returned to Nazareth in hopes of resuming normal life.

But we now know that was not God's plan. Sadly, in the accounts of the early church, we lose focus on Nazareth as a center of the early Christian faith as churches grew in Antioch, Alexandria,

Jerusalem, and Rome. History and archaeology inform us that early Christ-followers were dwelling in Nazareth in the fourth century and perhaps generations earlier.

But today the gospel in Nazareth is flowering anew from its ancient roots. This new and mighty work is being revealed in its churches, schools, and missions. Botrus Mansour, head of the Nazareth Baptist School, an attorney, an author plus blogger, challenges the coming generation to pick up their cross and follow Jesus in loving God and neighbor.

Botrus and I first met more than twenty years ago during one of my many reporting trips to the Middle East and Africa. In his first book, *When Your Neighbor is the Savior*, he shared his heart and vision for Nazareth, all of the Holy Land, and our world. In this new devotional book, *Looking from the Precipice*, he picks up where he left off. What is the pearl of great price that Botrus has found living inside the modern state of Israel as a Christian among many Israeli Jews and Muslims?

First, he realizes that we live today in deeply troubled times. Second, he beckons us, rather than spinning out narratives about the end of days, to turn our hearts again toward God and each other. This means building on the rock and not the shifting sand. It also means that Christian education and the integration of faith and learning are essential to individuals, families, churches, communities, and nations, regardless of their ethnicity, race, or creed.

This book ranges deeply and broadly into Christian devotion, discipleship, mission, current events, and the relationship between theology and practice. We Christians live in a world with more than two billion fellow disciples, and Botrus has an urgent message for the global church. His view from Nazareth has an ancient-future orientation. In Nazareth, there is Mary's well, the traditional site of the Annunciation, located a short distance away from many vibrant Catholic, Orthodox, and Protestant congregations, not to mention Christian schools and many other biblical institutions.

Botrus believes each generation should recommit itself to following Christ. This is the way to move forward because that's where we will meet Jesus again. His message is that the transforming gospel truly gives us sustainable hope for the future and today.

Every Christian disciple needs great instruction, but also a great example. Botrus models respectful dialogue and Gospel-based engagement with the hottest of hot-button issues. This confident posture gives me great hope that Christianity in the Holy Land will survive and thrive for generations to come. This book is a fresh voice from the same place—Nazareth—that at first responded to Jesus in disbelief. But today it challenges the world to love Jesus, know Jesus, and follow him.

Timothy C. Morgan
Director, Journalism Certificate program
Wheaton College (Illinois)

The Mount of Precipitation (Precipice) in Nazareth's southern end today is one of my favorite spots. It is a place where people come to pray, contemplate, and meditate away from the buzz of the town of Nazareth as well as look over the vast scene, especially to the south and sideways.

However, it is the place where the people of my hometown, Nazareth, seized Jesus 2,000 years ago in order to throw him from its cliff. According to tradition Jesus not only "walked right through the crowd and went on his way" (as the Bible states), but even jumped from the cliff and landed safely in the Jezreel valley below. Either way—the Precipitation is a place of rejection.

The angry people of Nazareth could not accept the fact that in his speech in the synagogue that day Jesus noted two Gentiles from the Old Testament as heroes of faith. They could not accept that his grace was available to every nation. Therefore, Precipitation is also a place of exclusivity.

Isn't the heart of the human race a Mount of Precipitation of its own?

Today, not only am I a citizen of Nazareth, but also the Lord has placed me in a distinct position and location: I belong to a tiny minority in Israel. I am an Arab, a Palestinian, a Christian, an Evangelical, and a citizen of Israel. These sub-identities have the potential to contradict one another.

I was raised as a son of the first Arab Palestinian Christian journalist in Israel who worked in an Israeli Hebrew newspaper. My dad was a Greek Melkite Catholic and my mom a Greek Orthodox. In different times of my life I attended Catholic,

Anglican, Baptist, and Jewish schools and universities with Arab Muslim and Christian children and Jewish students in Jerusalem and Nazareth. I then practiced law in both Jewish and Arab lawyers' firms. Later I started serving in my community in Nazareth as a director of the only recognized Evangelical school in Israel and as a church leader in different positions in Israel and abroad. Through all these experiences, I have interacted with Arab and Jewish people in Israel as well as with Evangelicals around the world.

Through the years I have mastered the skill of navigation among my sub-identities in interacting with these different people and in forming views on numerous loaded issues. However, my conviction is that the Lordship of Jesus should be the deciding factor in our stances, guiding us in overcoming and reconciling these contradictions.

God tells us that we are all his handiwork (Ephesians 2:10) and he has made us kings and priests (Revelation 1:6). Belonging to God is the identity that absorbs all other sub-identities. Our identity in God should surely *rule over* our other identities but not *rule them out*.

Nazareth's geographic location in the middle of the narrow strip of Israel provides a prime location for viewing the surroundings. Standing on the top of Precipice Mountain one can see Mount Carmel to the west, the Gilboa Mountains to the east-south, the Jezreel Valley beneath the mountain to the south, Megiddo (the Armageddon site) to the southwest, Mount Tabor (the site of the Transfiguration) to the southeast, the Jordan Valley to the east, and the town of Nazareth, as well as other biblical sites, to the north.

I have written numerous articles that reflect the tension among these sub-identities, others that address matters in the church both locally and internationally, as well as matters of interest in the community. Most were written in Arabic and just a few in Hebrew and English. I found it fitting to translate them into English for this book.

Some of the articles are related to a season in the church year, some are related to the inner life and soul, some address the life of the mind, and others speak to matters of the important work of churches in community. Some reflective questions have been added for pondering after each article.

Metaphorically, I aim to stand on the Precipice today and in a spirit of grace and inclusiveness look at the world and its complicated issues. May God help me. I pray this book will be of benefit to all who read it.

Part One

Seasons in the Life of the Church

How do we make ourselves accountable for a new year?

Each year as the calendar is about to turn, adding another number, people engage in celebrating the occasion. More importantly, however, we confront ourselves, asking, What lessons should I learn from the past year in order to plan for the future?

We cannot pursue a better future, progress, or success without understanding the past. Personal lessons are derived from past experiences. If the experience is positive, it is to be repeated (maybe with a few improvements), or if it is negative, one needs to refrain from such experiences in the future. Deriving lessons and making personal decisions for the New Year requires an honest retrospective look and a genuine bringing of oneself to account in order to correct mistakes, plan, and make decisions. Otherwise, how can one build a better future? If we build our future decisions based on an incorrect view of the past (by not holding ourselves accountable), future decisions will also be faulty.

Generally speaking, I believe most people find it difficult to bring themselves to account, either during the New Year season, or at any other time.

Our personal accountability system, in general, is flawed as it conflicts with our selfishness and self-interests. Past mistakes are often viewed as another person's fault. The reason behind any disappointment, conflict, loss, or failure is usually the other, not oneself. Perfection, truth, and honesty are usually on my side— and I end up free from blame.

Although this is gradually changing, there has been an absence of accountability in traditional Arab societies. One of the reasons behind this is that the identity and the history of Arabs have increased the probability of rejecting self-accountability. The negative image of Arabs in the eyes of other people has caused Arabs to adopt a defensive, solitary mentality and to reject self-accountability. Moreover, companies and governmental organizations in Arab societies have not been rooted in accountability due to the corrupt nature of their systems; cronyism in recruitment and promotions based on a family, tribal, or sectarian basis have continued to be dominant. All this has resulted in a mentality that has rejected accountability for personal actions. Thankfully, we have seen gradual change in recent years.

Accountability requires self-honesty, but how can people be honest with themselves when they are not honest with others? This dishonesty stems from a lack of security. People whose identity and position are well established do not hesitate to hold themselves accountable, no matter the cost.

The Lord Jesus set repentance, self-accountability, self-review, and confession as the main pillars of people's relationship with God. In contrast, the things he detested most were viewing oneself more highly than one ought to, pride, and self-righteousness. Therefore, our Lord praised the poor in spirit and condemned the spiritual pride of the Pharisees. He condemned the pride of the Pharisee shown in his self-righteous prayer but praised the humility of the tax collector who beat his breast, acknowledging his need for mercy. By his rich grace, the Lord alleviated the heavy burden of self-accountability when he added the concepts of forgiveness and acceptance and walking the second mile. The Lord loves those who bring themselves to account honestly and vow to change their ways, and then he blesses their new beginnings.

Do we transcend the worn-out, hollow general greetings, and bring ourselves to account sincerely to change our ways for the New Year?

Reflect

1. Consider two negative experiences you had in the past year. Write down what you learned from them and what you will do so as not to repeat them.

2. You've just read: "Our personal accountability system, in general, is flawed as it conflicts with our selfishness and self-interest." Do you agree?

How to wish a happy holiday season

When a holiday season arrives, people hasten to greet one another. In the past, people in our cities and villages used to pay visits to each other to bring wishes for a happy season. These were short visits to homes, where desserts and liquor were served. People also used to insist on visiting bereaved families on occasions like Christmas day or Easter Sunday.

Nowadays, all this has changed. It seems that due to the stresses of life, home visits on special occasions have decreased, and they have been replaced by less personal messages: electronic greetings. Some people just send their season's greetings to everyone at once, via public Facebook status updates, Facebook messages, or emails. There are also text messages sent to all contacts. People now greet their friends, acquaintances, and family members using a one-sentence greeting. Nevertheless, greetings and wishes on special seasons and occasions (even if via text) help to maintain social relationships when they are expressed from the heart and they show care and love.

I wonder what greetings or wishes mean: are they just to wish good for the other person, or are they a prayer to God concerning my neighbor? Have my wishes become mechanical, so that I just say them without thinking of their meaning? Or are they as rich in meaning as they ever were, just now taking on a new form?

This year, I wondered whether I should send out electronic greetings. If so, what would I write so that they become special, expressive, and personal, and to avoid their being disagreeable or ordinary? Here were some options I came up with.

1. *Using a common greeting: Best wishes for the holiday season!*

Reasoning: It is good to wish the other person "the best." Wishing or praying for "the best" for another person feels noble. God is good and he is the source of all good. We can enjoy the best things in life with the help and blessing of God.

2. *Greeting by quoting a Bible verse.*

Reasoning: I love the idea of using God's living Word to greet others. For instance, this verse from Isaiah on Christmas has powerful words that show the Lord's glory:

> For to us a child is born, to us a son is given, and the government will be on his shoulders. And he will be called Wonderful Counselor, Mighty God, Everlasting Father, Prince of Peace. (Isaiah 9:6)

And on New Year's Eve, the verse that is commonly cited is: "You crown the year with your bounty, and your carts overflow with abundance" (Psalm 65:11).

Quoting Bible verses is an expression of our love of the Word of God, and it contributes to the spread of the Word to others. On the other hand, quoting these verses, though they are beautiful and powerful, lacks a personal touch in the message you are communicating. It also can limit creativity.

3. *Using a funny greeting.*

Reasoning: Some people quickly find funny, light, and rhyming statements that are widespread on the internet to copy. For example, I received one that said: "There are several types of coffee: the mild one like your lighthearted soul, the strong one like your wise mind, the sweet one like your graceful face, the bitter one like your absence, and the medium strength one that is like meeting you in person." Such statements leave a smile on your face, but the reader likely knows they are just copied and not personal.

4. Writing a personal greeting from the heart. Wishing for peace, health, joy, and numerous blessings of the Lord.

Reasoning: I like being personal. I tried to belong to this group, but among thousands of greetings, I wrestled with being distinct and creative to all of my recipients to touch their hearts.

I may struggle with this question every year. However, for me, what it comes down to is that the best greeting, wish, and prayer that I could ever offer someone on a special occasion (creative or not) is to be in the will of God in the New Year, where there is goodness, peace, and true success. Let it be known to you that seeking these things away from his will is mere illusion. I pray for all those whom I am greeting, that we will be in God's will this year!

Reflect

1. What are some distinctive traditions in your culture for New Year's celebrations, Easter, and Christmas?
2. How might you be more creative and write a seasonal greeting for each holiday that focuses on what is important?

Valentines and Divine love

People from different religions call Christianity "the religion of love." Some call it so because they admire its superiority, but others call it so out of disregard because, for them, treating others with love in a world of cruelty and ferocity is impossible. They say: How can we love as the Bible requires us to do (loving our enemies) in a world that hates, harms, plots with evil, and fights?

The truth is that the whole world is based on love, and without love we slide into rigidity, dryness, and deadly wilderness. With love, we experience joy, creativity, and sacrifice.

Someone once challenged me to find a movie that does not revolve around love, and truly I did not find any. All movies tackle love: romantic love, patriotic love, self-love, motherly love, family love, love for science, love for religion, love for nature, and more. As movies, in general, are a reflection of life, it is difficult for us to imagine life without love.

The whole world celebrates Valentine's Day on the 14th of February. Men hasten to buy their wives or girlfriends flowers. Clothes shops and jewelry stores are crowded with people buying gifts to present to their loved one.

Lovers write words of love on cards to send as a letter, or text messages on cell phones, or Facebook messages and posts of affection.

This holiday celebrates love, but each person may be celebrating a different kind of love. Is it the loyal, humble, engaging love that serves the other partner and is connected to one's destiny forever, in days of happiness and calamity? Or is it a love based on admiration of outer appearance, wild imagination, romantic feelings, and temporary pleasure? Is it a constant, stable love or a changing, inconsistent one?

In the purest sense, it is a compliment when people call our Christian faith "the religion of love." As the Bible says, "God is love" (1 John 4:16b), and all that God has said or done has been immersed in his ocean of love.

God has implanted in his superior creation, human beings, the instinct of love. The spring of love has flowed into the hearts of his creation.

Undoubtedly, for every kind of love, there is a stage of maturity. Regarding the love of the other gender, it starts in a male's life by, for instance, his love for his mother, then his female teacher, then his kind classmate, then his beautiful neighbor, then the charming young woman he meets in the neighborhood or at church, then his attractive friend at university, then his fiancée who then becomes his wife, then his daughter, ending hopefully and God willing with his granddaughter. This list is not a recipe, and the types of love vary greatly; its order may change, and some figures on the list may not be there at the different stages of life. But each age has its special kind of love.

How can we evaluate the type of love we are experiencing so that we come to the best and finest of them all? The best way is to ask about its cost.

The most expensive love in the universe is the one that caused our glorious God to abandon the right hand of greatness, to come in the flesh, dwell among us, walk to the cross, and die there for the sake of humankind. A drop of blood from the side of our glorious Lord hanging on the cross is the highest price ever paid for love. This love is more expensive than all the treasures on earth. It is a sacrificial love of the Creator and sustainer of the universe by his powerful word.

This love penetrates the soul and then flows out to others. It is a love that desires good for others because it comes from the God of all goodness; it is of a divine source, and so it touches souls tenderly as it comes from the source of all tenderness.

Some people might object to this, saying we should not mix Valentine's Day with the love of God; there is nothing in common between them. We answer those by saying, the source of all good and love is the Lord our God, as he has put such instinct of love in us, and we should never ignore it. We are calling for placing this love in its right context, celebrating it as derived from the river of God's love.

I am always moved by the words of the Arabic worship song entitled "The Story of Wondrous Love," especially the verse that reads:

Every love in the universe stems from the love of Jesus, every love in my being is a return of the love of Jesus.

Whoever prepares themselves to be a vessel ready to be filled with Divine love will certainly be used for good, and love will flow from their heart to the whole world, whether on Valentine's Day or any other day of the year.

Reflect
1. What do you define as love?
2. Can you think of other ways to evaluate love, beyond those suggested here?

A stream of love springs on Golgotha

Consider the events of that dark day in Jerusalem. The Father presented his Son, who is not only a beloved son but the Lord of the universe, the one who partakes in divinity through the Trinity since eternity. The Father allowed the Son to be hit by the sword of death and to be stabbed by soldiers with a spear on Golgotha as he hung between earth and heaven, for no sin he had committed. The hearts of the Father and the Son were broken because of their separation on the cross in the greatest love story history has ever known, or will ever know.

The daughters of Jerusalem cried over their beloved, while the soldiers led him to be crucified with humiliation. We weep today as we remember this dreadful scene. We grieve, cry, and fast, with much passion: who can hold oneself back upon seeing the sinless one, who has no deceit in his mouth, being led to crucifixion?

However, the cross is more than just a scene that stirs emotions. It is the central scene in the history of humankind; it is the time when the crucified connected earth and heaven. At that time Christ, who knew no sin, was made a curse and a sin for us. By this the Son restored to the fold whoever believes in the Father.

Above all, God's indescribable love was demonstrated on the cross. On this cross of contempt, God's greatest love was manifested, as the cost was the highest ever—the shed blood of the Son of God.

In front of this indescribable love, everything changes. Through the cross, humans are reconciled with their God and Creator. The cross restores us to our original state: to the intimate relationship with our Creator, who created us in his image. That image was distorted because of our deviation, which made it difficult to experience this likeness with God's image. However, the cross restored what had been stolen and fixed all that had been distorted.

The cross encourages us to remember the basics. For instance, we remember that the origin of everything is love, as God is love. As a loving, innovative Creator, he created us to be in an intimate, loving relationship with him. God has implanted in his creation a stream of love. Humanity longs for this kind of love. It is like a mirage that it continues to pursue for a lifetime, hoping to find it.

Through the cross, the Lord has removed all that hinders or damages our relationship, the disobedience of humankind by sinning. Heaven showered humans with love so that human hearts overflowed with it—a wellspring that won't be drained.

We wandered in the dry wilderness, but with the freshness of the overflowing spring, the thirst for love came to an end. Now, we may drink from it until we are filled.

Reflect

1. How do the symbols of that day on Golgotha relate to the symbols in your life?
2. How was the cross the means to reconnect earth and heaven?

No matter how they diminish Easter

Easter has not been named "the big feast" haphazardly. It is big because of the meaning of its events for the world, starting from the very first Adam until the last of Adam's descendants that live on this earth.

But several factors have diminished the value of Easter in my country, and even in our Arab churches.

Christian inhabitants are less than two percent of the population of Israel. This makes Easter of little influence on the public atmosphere. Things then become even worse because Christians do not unite in setting the feast's date. In places where more than half a population identifies as Christian, this difference doesn't register as important—but here in Israel, it does. When one group is shouting "Hosanna" and carrying palm fronds, another will be greeting each other with "Christ is risen. He has risen indeed." Because there are different dates for celebrating Easter, Christians in Nazareth rarely have the opportunity to feel as if they are celebrating together. Instead, they find out that one of every six people in town have already celebrated, and one in six will be celebrating next week or even few weeks later, according to the respective year's calendar.

Easter also lacks a certain local popular charm. To this, you can probably relate, no matter where you live. At Christmas, the hero is a child for whom the Magi brought precious gifts from the East, and thus it's the feast of gifts and decorations, and Santa Claus and has found strong popular roots far and wide. But Easter is an occasion of passion, grief, a cross, a betrayal, a trial, and treachery. Therefore, if you do not understand the purpose behind its grave calamities, it will mean nothing to you. If you do not understand that behind the pain there is redemption, and behind the sorrow there is breakthrough and salvation, you will never really be able to interact with it in a meaningful way.

Several years ago, I happened to be on board a US domestic flight on Good Friday. When the plane was about to land at O'Hare Airport, Chicago, I naively expected the pilot to wish the passengers a blessed Easter. Am I not in the most Christian country in the developed world? I was surprised that the captain did not utter a word regarding the occasion but sufficed to wish a great weekend to all!

Christians in the West seem also not to give much significance to Easter. This minimization of its public and popular role is unfortunately being copied to the feast's features in the Middle East.

The synchronization of Christian Easter and the Jewish Passover (*Pesach*) in Israel affects the former and places it in a secondary position in a country ruled by a Jewish majority. Jews celebrate their crossing from slavery in Egypt to freedom; but as for the religious celebrations of the minority, these are surely marginalized.

Despite this marginalization and diminishing of Easter, a true believer will always hold Easter sacred and celebrate this holiest of weeks. It is the most important week that has ever happened and will ever happen in the history of humanity. God sent his only Son to die on the cross like a criminal! Every person past and present should have died and been sent to hell in eternal separation from God, who created them. If this had happened, it would have been the greatest human tragedy, but it would have been just.

The Lord Jesus came to our world and accepted, out of his wonderful and gracious love, to pay the whole penalty on the cross to prevent this tragedy and provide deliverance and a way of rescue for whoever believes in him.

I remember all this during Passion Week. I will celebrate the Cross and the Resurrection, and I will delight in them no matter how the outside world tries to diminish the occasion.

Reflect

Why does Easter commemorate the central part of our faith, and not Christmas?

The story of wondrous Love

People are calling out for "love," lifting it to the highest position. They seek it, pursue it, and sacrifice precious things for it. Love stirs creativity, work, activity, and devotion. Loving one's nation is the fuel for building it up. For years loving God has driven people to leave their homes behind and travel to serve others. A mother's love for her children makes her work day and night to secure their comfort. As for self-love, it is the cause of wars and fighting. Sometimes, strong love drives people to sacrifice themselves for the sake of what they understand to be patriotism, or love for God. Love is truly as strong as death!

Yet, the true example of love is God himself, and the best, the strongest, and the greatest type of love is God's love.

God's love is enormous in measure, quality, design, and manifestation. It causes us to stand still and wonder as our human minds fail to comprehend its secrets and depths.

This love is demonstrated in four elements: the identity and nature of the loving God, the identity of each person whom God loves, the quality and depth of this love, and the cost paid for this love.

1. The identity and nature of the loving God.

This leaves us in awe and fear of his majesty, strength, and eternal power. God is creator of the vast universe and its minute details (Job 38:4). He is the sustainer of all things by his powerful word (Hebrews 1:3). He is the everlasting God; all-sufficient, the Beginning and the End. He is the way, the truth, the life, and the gate. He has never been an ordinary king, and kings of the earth are like dust at his feet. One word from our loving God can make this universe come to an end and be completely ruined.

2. *The identity of each person whom God loves.*

We are small, weak, limited, and sinful, placing ourselves in the center, rebelling against God our creator, cursing him, and disobeying his commands. We show such arrogance toward the creator, even though a small disorder in our heart may easily kill us (or a COVID-19 virus as we have so clearly experienced), and a few degrees increase in our body temperature may end our days. A minute delay in the movement of the earth in its orbit, an earthquake, a hurricane, or an increase in temperature exposes our lives to utter vulnerability. Despite this excessive fragility and the fact that we depend on God to continue living, we raise our heads and challenge God.

Then we ignore God in our daily life—until a storm of failure, a health crisis, or a family quarrel takes place, and then we heap accusations against God as the cause of our problems! This is our nature: ungrateful, untrustworthy, sinful. All of humankind is the same; all are, without exception, rebellious against God, though we differ in the level and extent of our rebellion.

3. *The quality and depth of love of this great, mighty God who created us and gave us life, even though we continue to sin against him.*

God did not wait for humanity to perish because of our evil, but abandoned his throne in heaven and became incarnate as an infant human, born in a manger in Palestine two thousand years ago to save wretched humankind. This was the only way to fulfill God's justice; God is the Holy One who hates sin.

4. *The cost paid for this love. Justice demands humanity's death for sinning against God.*

However, God desires life for humankind, his creation, and out of his love that passes understanding he decided to pay the cost himself. He lived on our earth, walked to the cross and on the cross, and the sinless One died. Thus, he fulfilled justice's requirements. On the cross, God's sentence was carried out and his wonderful love was demonstrated. On the cross, both the fulfillment of God's justice and his great love were clearly demonstrated. The Son of God died on the cross and shed his noble blood, paying the cost of our sins.

By the death of God's Son, God has composed the song of the greatest love story history has ever seen or ever will see. It is the story of indescribable love whose greatness is measured by the greatness of its giver (the God of the universe), by the identity of the recipient (fallen, ungrateful humans), by its quality, and by its paid price. It is a divine initiative, and its cost was the death of the Son of God.

Do you love him in return for all that he has done for you?

Reflect

What are the four elements that reflect God's love, and how can you be reminded of them daily?

Contradictions from the Annunciation to the Resurrection

How strange the story of Christianity is!

It started with the incarnation of the Giver of Life himself in the womb of a humble girl. He was not born of human seed, but by a miracle from God. Not only was his chosen mother a humble girl, but she was from a marginalized village in forgotten, good-for-nothing Galilee.

He had a miraculous start to life, and a lowly birth. The cornerstone himself was born in a poor manger in Bethlehem. Shortly afterward, Joseph and Mary took the King of Kings in their arms and ran away from the assault of a tyrannical, bloody king to find refuge in Egypt.

Then, the One who sat at the right hand of the Father grew up in the lowlife town of Nazareth, running and playing in its narrow alleys. When the keeper of secrets of heaven and earth started his ministry, he chose simple and ordinary men and women to follow him. While the creator of the universe wandered in Galilee, Judea, and Samaria, he did not have a place to lay his head. All the while, his teachings tipped the scales. Jesus called people to be poor in spirit instead of seeking power, to be meek instead of domineering, to be merciful instead of hardhearted, and to be peacemakers instead of war launchers. The Son of God encouraged people to love their enemies instead of hating them, as well as to pray and fast in secret instead of publicly.

This series of contradictions did not stop even during the last week of Jesus's life on earth: the victorious judge of the world started the week by entering Jerusalem riding a donkey instead of a horse as conquerors and invaders of cities do.

A few days later, the sustainer of all things rented a place to eat a Passover meal with his disciples. During the supper, the Lord of Lords wrapped a towel around his waist and bowed down to wash the dirty feet of his disciples, modeling the humility that he taught. The one whose love for us led him to the death of the cross did not find a single person to stay up with him or join him in prayer on the night before he was nailed to the cross.

On the same night, the soldiers arrested Jesus, even though he was the one who called for the release of captives. Judas, the traitor, betrayed the most faithful person of all with a deceitful kiss. Although the Lord of hosts could have summoned battalions of angels to rescue him from this brutal attack, he voluntarily surrendered himself to his enemies—for our sake.

The religious and political leadership in Jerusalem falsely sentenced to death the One who will judge humanity. The soldiers humiliated and made fun of the One of all majesty, glory, and everlasting power. The closest of his disciples denied him three times in front of a maid, forgetting that his master is faithful. The most righteous One was raised on the cross of shame between criminals. There, they twisted for him a crown of thorns instead of laurel, while instead crowns of glory should have been laid at his feet. They gave him vinegar to drink, even though he is the spring of living water to all people. And then, the corpse of the creator and preserver of all things had no place to be buried, so a rich man lent him a grave.

This story of contradictions, that no one could ever invent, came to an unexpected end three days later when he rose again from the grave: our living God rose victoriously and defeated death. What an amazing end to Jesus's life on earth! From the hands of humans, he endured oppression, pain, and murder. He replaced all these with life.

Similarly, as was true 2,000 years ago, Eastern Christians nowadays feel helpless as they are greatly suffering from the tyranny of harsh criminals on one side, and the inaction of authorities and the scramble of silent conspirators on the other. Yet, as we are encouraged a little with the stand of our noble Muslim neighbors, we find true comfort that the dawn of Resurrection is surely coming. The God who seemed helpless will rise with victory early on Sunday, defaming death and conquering it. By his death, he will grant us life, and by his resurrection, he will raise us from the dead.

Sunday is near for those who await it. Happy Easter to all!

Reflect

1. Think of the contradictions in the life of Jesus. How are they contradictions?
2. Can you think of any other contradictions in the life of Jesus?

The dawn of the third day is coming

Easter often comes to Middle Eastern Arab Christians with certain worries. In Egypt, Christians await the future pessimistically because of the growth of the fundamentalist political parties' power. In Syria, which has experienced a bloody civil war for a decade, most Christians supported President Bashar El-Assad because of his provision of relative safety and security. Now, years later, they are in fear of the future that might be ruled by Muslim violent fanatic groups. And then there is the fear that comes with chaos, which seems to reign even more these days. The circumstances of Arab Christians in the rest of the Middle Eastern countries are by no means better.

While we reflect on the events of Passion Week, Jesus and his disciples during that week were seemingly just like Eastern Arab Christians of the present era.

At the beginning of Holy Week, Jesus entered Jerusalem riding a borrowed donkey, while war heroes at that time used to ride horses in victory parades—a symbol of pride, strength, and vigor. Eastern Christians today ride a donkey, metaphorically, of meekness, patience, and humility. They are forced into this because of their position as a persecuted minority.

The conspiracy to kill Jesus was being plotted as the chief priests were fed up with him. They decided to arrest him cunningly, so they dedicated thirty pieces of silver to secure his arrest. They succeeded in their plan, as they found a traitor among his disciples. Maybe there is no conspiracy against Christians to have the Middle East free of Christians, but it seems that there are social and political affairs that crack down on them. It is the atmosphere of intolerance, hatred, and conflict that leads to the elimination of Christians in the Middle East, either by killing them, or by pushing them to emigrate from the land of their ancestors. This has already happened in Lebanon, Palestine, Iraq, Egypt, and Syria. Where next? Where are we supposed to go?

Judas became a guide to the soldiers who arrested Jesus, betraying him with a kiss, and so Jesus was brought to an unjust trial filled with false testimony, oppression, and lying. Thus, he was sentenced to crucifixion. Christians in Middle Eastern countries today are often treated unfairly and in a biased fashion. In some countries there are restrictions on building churches and on freedom of worship for those who follow Christ. In other countries, Christians' civil rights go unrecognized, and there is blatant discrimination against them.

Jesus's disciples panicked and so they scattered. Judas the treasurer had betrayed Jesus, and Peter the brave disciple denied him in front of three different groups of people. Because of persecution, many Eastern Christians have felt forced to compromise their faith. They have divided into parties and denominations, and they have been weakened by these awful circumstances.

Jesus was taken to the cross, and only a few women remained with him. The heavenly Father hid his face from him, so Jesus shouted: "My God, My God, why have you forsaken me?" This is a situation where one feels estranged and lonely, without a companion, whether in heaven or on earth. Middle Eastern Christians often have the feeling of loneliness and isolation. We are a tiny minority throughout the region. In some situations, our Muslim brothers turn their backs on us. At other times, Christians in the rest of the world are distracted by their own affairs and are unaware of Middle Eastern Christians' dilemmas.

The sun had darkened, and Jesus died a horrible death on the cross with criminals. The disciples were scattered, and everyone thought that the story had come to an end. Was it a crushing defeat? In the same way, it seems that Christians in our East have had a crushing defeat and that history has turned the page against them.

However, the third day witnessed the greatest declaration of all: "He is not here, but he has risen"! Jesus defeated death and he rose triumphantly! He paid the cost of the sins of mankind and redeemed us from the fist of Satan, assuring this by the seal of his glorious resurrection. The third day will come in the life of Middle Eastern Christians, too. We will see an empty tomb and we will experience the power of his resurrection in our lives if we have faith in the victorious Lord.

Christ has risen! He has risen indeed!

Reflect

1. What are some trials and challenges that Christians in your part of the world are facing?
2. How can you be hopeful regarding those difficulties as you ponder Jesus's victory over death?

A week in Jesus's life if he lived in today's world

Monday

Media and press agencies have reported that a person from Galilee is performing strange healing miracles around the district of Tiberias. Citizens from all over the country have flocked to Tiberias upon hearing the news. The traffic congestion spreads from Puria junction to Beit Ramon junction.

Prof. Rosenberg, Head of the Medical Doctors' Union in Israel, stated, "Up to this moment, there is no medical explanation for the cures of chronic diseases that are reported to have been performed by this person." A *Haaretz* correspondent in the north reported that the person involved in performing the strange healings comes from the city of Nazareth, but this information was unable to be verified by press time.

Tuesday

As reported yesterday, strange events continue to take place in the country. Following the news of healings taking place for different kinds of sickness in Tiberias yesterday, our correspondents reported stranger news today, but this time in Tel Aviv. The person whose name was linked with the healings was seen providing meals for thousands of people at Hayarkon Park in Tel Aviv. The entity supporting that campaign was not known, but the person involved at the center of the activity was named Jesus the Nazarene.

One would expect that a person doing miraculous healing would be a finely dressed doctor who only specializes in healing one type of disease. But our reports state that Jesus the Nazarene looked like an ordinary man, was dressed in shabby clothes, and was feeding, talking to, and healing everyone.

Some volunteers helped him in distributing the meals, serving the multitudes gently. The distributed meals consisted of a single hamburger in a fresh loaf of Arabic bread, salad, and fries.

Some eyewitnesses have mentioned that the Nazarene spoke about the kingdom of God before providing the meals, causing public interest and joy except for some rabbis in the area. Juda Zaken, the manager of McDonald's, reported to our correspondent that providing meals in such a manner stopped the flow of clients to his restaurant that day. He declared that his staff also received a free meal and they were totally satisfied.

Wednesday

The government is meeting to discuss how to respond to the accusations of Jesus the Nazarene brought against the Prime Minister, the Minister of National Security, the Minister of Social Affairs, and the Minister of Housing. Some ministries expressed their astonishment at the accuracy of the information shown on Channel 2 yesterday regarding embezzlement from the budget of the Bank of Housing, sexual abuses that took place at the Ministry of Social Affairs and the Prime Minister's office, and acts of oppression and torture against citizens of Halhul in the West Bank permitted by the Minister of National Security.

Defense lawyers of the accused denied all the accusations against the Prime Minister and other ministers. They refused to provide any explanations for the documented information submitted by the Nazarene and reported by Channel 2.

Amnon Abravomich, the senior political commentator of Channel 2, mentioned that he could not recall such a detailed and revealing report since the establishment of the state, adding that such reports raise the banner of integrity at a time of deterioration of values in the country.

Thursday

A group of famous correspondents and reporters of Al-Jazeera, Al-Arabiya, CNN, BBC, and other channels arrived in the country to cover the phenomenon of "the Nazarene."

In an exclusive interview with Al-Jazeera, the Nazarene said that we should love our enemies. He added that he has been sent to the world to redeem humankind from the penalty of sin. Commentators disagreed among themselves about this phenomenon and the new teaching of the Nazarene.

In Nazareth, a march started from Mary's well to the main city square in support of their fellow citizen who was the subject of attacks by different political figures.

Friday

The Nazarene Phenomenon has spread all over the world. Tens of thousands of new groups have formed on Facebook for discussing it. Most people doubt his credibility but quite a number are encouraging Facebook users to believe him and follow him. People are wondering why we don't see the Nazarene himself using social media to spread his message.

Presidents and prime ministers of several countries around the world, including the president of the US, are trying to reach the Nazarene, so far without success.

Some of his close friends (they call themselves "disciples") have spoken to states' leaders and expressed their views. Correspondents accompanying the charismatic leader have reported that he spends most days healing the sick, as well as speaking and laughing with children.

Sources close to the disciples report that the Nazarene recently spent an evening at a wedding in Cana of Galilee. He gently rebuked the hosts of the wedding for eating too much and throwing away huge amounts of leftovers. Then, he prayed, and miraculously, the food was packed in special thermostatic boxes to keep it fresh. The disciples of the Nazarene then distributed the boxes to citizens of nearby villages, and the guests of the wedding enjoyed their food and the nice party.

Saturday

Reliable sources state that the Nazarene spent his weekend with his family in Nazareth out of the spotlight, and he spoke about his imminent death to redeem humankind. During his stay in the city, he met with his disciples and gave them some guidelines and instructions. He encouraged them to love one another. They asked him about various topics but he, above all, stressed loving one another.

Sunday

The Nazarene, who we now understand is known as Jesus of Nazareth, or Jesus Christ, set his sight on his mission and went to Jerusalem very early in the morning to spend there the most important week in his life on earth.

Indeed, it was the most important week in our lives as well.

Reflect

1. Use your imagination to think of another situation that would have occurred if Jesus had lived in our age, in your context.
2. Do you think that Jesus's core message and mission would have changed if the setting of his incarnation had changed?

Terror did not pass on the first Easter

Easter is the week of anguish culminating in the crucifixion and resurrection of Jesus from the dead. The sad week includes betrayal, a false trial, the frightened dispersion of the disciples of Jesus, the repudiation of Peter—senior among his disciples— the humiliating procession to Calvary, and the agony on the cross between two criminals, leading to Jesus's death.

But the week begins on the Sunday of the palms: the entrance of Jesus to Jerusalem as a king riding on a donkey with the audience waving palm branches and spreading their clothes on the ground along his route. Every Christian family in the Middle East recognizes this as a happy holiday in which the children wear their best, most colorful clothes, and mothers compete with each other to prepare the most beautiful *Sha'nini* that their children will hold during the traditional procession after the Mass. This *"Sha'nini"* began as bare palm branches and later became palm branches combined with beautiful flowers or candles decorated with flowers. In Arabic, the verb *Yesha'nin* was also invented (in the sense of celebrating the Palm Festival), and participation became a kind of folk celebration for each child. Then the children star in the pictures their parents post to various social media outlets.

Palm Sunday has, in recent years, been a frightening time. Coptic Christian families from Tanta, north of Cairo and Alexandria, celebrated Palm Sunday in April 2017, and before they finished their prayers, the long arm of ISIS arrived. Two brainwashed and inhumane terrorists murdered forty-four people, including women and children.

There were waves of trembling and noise in the Arab world in general and among Christians in particular when news of the two attacks on the holiday day spread. The persistence of the murderousness of ISIS and its ilk, and the government's helplessness, caused distress and despair. Egypt is considered the largest Arab country. The land of the Nile is the Oracle, culturally and religiously, as the Arab Christians that live in it, by a conservative estimate, are about ten million (twice the number of the rest of Christians in the Middle East). The attacks in Egypt added to the sense of Christians that they are rejected in the region, and especially in Iraq and Syria: in the former, hundreds of thousands were exiled after the fall of Saddam Hussein, and in the latter, Christians are the weakest link in their bloody war.

In the days of Nasser's Arab nationalism, many Christians found refuge in Egypt as representing a common denominator for all Arabs. In the days of the Soviet Union and the Eastern Bloc, many Christians crowded around Communism, calling for class equality and the rejection of religion, every religion. With the collapse of these, Christians remained in a broken trough. Those who could do so emigrated. Some of those that remain still embrace the glorious days of Pan-Arab secularism, some live in despair and devote their time to their homes, and some connect to the lesser of the evils, expressed by "moderate" dictators who fight against the violence of militant fundamentalist Islam.

In the meantime, Christians in Israel view the situation with mixed feelings: on the one hand, their security and economic situation are better than those of their Christian brothers and sisters in Arab countries, but on the other hand, they suffer, like their Muslim brothers, from the inequality and racism in the country.

After the joyous crowd called out Jesus's name when he entered Jerusalem on Palm Sunday, the angry clerics demanded that Jesus order them to remain silent. Christians now take comfort in his response and regard it as having a contemporary meaning: "If they keep quiet, the stones will cry out" (Luke 19:40b). The terror that did not pass over them at Easter silenced them, but hope still exists with the resurrection of their Savior from the dead.

Reflect

1. Why is it especially painful to witness people killed during worship?
2. How are the events of Holy Week a source of comfort for hurting Christians around the world?

An inseparable crimson cord between the cradle and Calvary

Celebrating Christmas in our country is becoming more popular. It is not limited to Christian believers anymore, but it is becoming an inclusive holiday that nominal Christians and even those from different religions celebrate. Celebrations have greatly expanded "The Grand Feast," replacing Easter in importance. For instance, the inauguration of the "Christmas Market" characterizes the season in Nazareth in mid-December. Tens of thousands of people visit, and two huge Christmas trees are decorated with lights: one next to the Greek Orthodox Annunciation Church, followed by the lighting of another for Roman Catholics near Benedictus Hall.

Christmas has become a popular joyful occasion. All people like this season, as it celebrates the birth of a poor child born in harsh conditions. The atmosphere of Christmas is comfortable, and this raises doubts for some of us, as the character of Jesus is generally controversial, everywhere and at all times. People still argue whether or not he was what he claimed to be, the Son of God. Just as important: Is the adult Jesus, the controversial historic character, different from the baby Jesus in the manger, loved and pitied by all?

While all gather around the cradle, we see the crowds scatter when the cross is set up. Thus, Easter week has not gained the same popularity and inclusiveness as Christmas, for it is the season of pain, passion, bitterness, conspiracies, the trial, and the grave. While people run to receive a meek child into our world, they refrain from attending funerals and dreadful situations.

While Christmas is lovable for its flowing joy, most tend to stay away from the Easter season they find melancholic.

Who do people prefer, the shepherds who rush to see the royal baby, or Judas, the sly, frowning traitor who got the thirty silver coins? Do they prefer the brightly lit shiny tree or the dry post on which Jesus was crucified? Do they prefer the Magi with their beautiful hats and valuable gifts or the scattered disciples and the denying Peter? Which is preferable, a guiding star in the sky or total darkness for three hours?

People prefer the scene of the Virgin Mary looking tenderly to her baby boy rather than her compassionate gaze upon her son lifted on the shameful cross.

The truth is that nobody will gather for Easter except those who believe that Good Friday is followed by a victorious Resurrection Sunday. Easter week is when God's profound provision to save humankind is embodied and Christian theology is focused. Without it, the heart of Christianity is taken out.

The main purpose of Jesus (and some will insist on it being his only goal) was to die for us. From the moment he was born as the child of Bethlehem, we see the foundation of the cross; the cross was planted in that cradle.

The weeping of the heavens together with the Marys who were next to the cross surpassed the crying of the baby after the birth pangs. Christmas is meaningless without the Crucifixion. His birth was not the birth of an ordinary child, even if it happened in exceptional circumstances and to a family we now regard as noble. We see the Incarnation through Christmas, and the incarnation of God was meant for the redemption for humanity. This is the inseparable cord between the cradle of Bethlehem and the cross of Calvary; do not try to cut it.

Reflect

1. What is this crimson inseparable cord? And why is it "crimson"?
2. Can you see the roots of the Passion in the birth of Jesus?

The paradox of the Day of Atonement and cycling

The Day of Atonement (*Yom Kippur* in Hebrew) has a profound religious and spiritual significance to the Jewish people. It is a feast in which Jews ask for forgiveness of their sins committed throughout the year. It was associated in the Old Testament with the entry of the High Priest into the place known as the "Holy of Holies" of the Temple. There, he offered animal sacrifices for both himself and the people. Ever since the Temple was destroyed in the first century, animal sacrifices have no longer been offered. During Yom Kippur, today, Jews pray and fast.

According to our Christian faith, every need for prayer and fasting was satisfied by the great sacrifice offered by God through his Son Jesus Christ, who bore the sins of the whole world. All sacrifices up until that point had been used to cover up certain sins and for a certain time, so that the offering of sacrifices had to be repeated every year. These sacrifices were symbols of what in the sacrifice of Jesus became the complete Sacrifice that will last forever—the redemption of the cross.

The author of the book of Hebrews explained:

But when Christ came as high priest of the good things that are now already here, he went through the greater and more perfect tabernacle that is not made with human hands, that is to say, is not a part of this creation. He did not enter by means of the blood of goats and calves; but he entered the Most Holy Place once for all by his own blood, thus obtaining eternal redemption. The blood of goats and bulls and the ashes of a heifer sprinkled on those who are ceremonially unclean sanctify them so that they are outwardly clean. How much more, then, will the blood of Christ, who through the eternal Spirit offered himself unblemished to God, cleanse our consciences from acts that lead to death, so that we may serve the living God! For this reason Christ is the mediator of a new covenant, that those who are called may receive the promised eternal inheritance—now that he has died as a ransom to set them free from the sins committed under the first covenant. (Hebrews 9:11–15)

However, you cannot ignore the paradoxes, entertaining or serious, between the religious significance of Yom Kippur, the Jewish application of it, and the popular meaning of the relationship with Palestinians who live in the land of Israel today.

For the ordinary Arab, Yom Kippur is the day of bicycles. It's just one day a year for cycling. In general, the culture of cycling does not exist in our societies. Our country is mountainous, the streets are narrow, the means of transportation are many, and the culture of reckless drivers makes cycling on regular days complicated and dangerous. However, on Yom Kippur, the Jewish inhabitants are grounded in their homes to pray and fast, and they refrain from any activity outside. As a result, Arab youth start cycling in groups in the streets that are empty of vehicles. Their bicycles have been polished for this day, so that their luster reaches out to Jewish cities such as Nazareth Illit (Nof Hagalil), as the young people play in the streets.

And as the opportunity to ride bikes in vacant streets on Yom Kippur increases, so does the theft of bicycles increase on that day. I know of a family whose daughter's bike was stolen, and as a joke, they consoled themselves by saying that if they were Jews, the sacrifice for Yom Kippur would have been the stolen bike.

The day of Yom Kippur reveals to us a high-quality surreal scene. It is the scene of the organized, modern, and developed Jewish city toward which Arabs usually look enviously and heartbreakingly, comparing it to their cities and their undeveloped, underfunded, chaotic villages. These Jewish cities are free for us—only one day a year—as Jews remain at home, fasting and praying, asking for forgiveness of their sins (a portion of which were committed against Arabs). Arabs go out to the streets to practice their annual day of cycling. The streets become playing courts and wide-open playgrounds. For one day only, the city becomes like an amusement park for Arab children, while the owners and masters of the city stay at home for the sake of their religion. This might be considered a glimpse of divine justice under the sponsorship of Yom Kippur as Arab kids are the ones "enjoying" the city's empty streets. Jews grieve and fast while Arabs rejoice and play in vacant Jewish streets.

The surrealistic scene of the Jewish cities is meant just for symbolism and fun, but there is another paradox: Israel closes the border crossing and strictly controls that closure during its feasts, including the Day of Atonement. In this way, Israel imposes confinement on Palestinians in the West Bank, where those areas are already restricted and neglected, preventing Palestinians from traveling or moving while the Jews are at home in prayer.

Another paradox is related to the Temple where the Al-Aqsa Mosque was built on its ruins. According to Jewish law the forgiveness of sins is complete by offering sacrifices in the Temple—which is not currently available at all. However, the most religious and fanatical Jewish groups are those who are calling for the destruction of Al-Aqsa Mosque so that they can fulfill the religious obligations of the Day of Atonement (and other religious rituals) in the Temple on that site. Does it make sense that the forgiveness of their sins "so that God is pleased with them" will happen when hundreds of millions of Muslims in the world are harmed and in pain?

These paradoxes remind all of us, of all religions and denominations and not just Jews and Arab Christians, that God desires us to do good and justice. God is not pleased with rituals, feasts, fasting, and prayer that are void of true repentance. As the prophet Isaiah said:

> Your New Moon feasts and your appointed festivals I hate with all my being. They have become a burden to me; I am weary of bearing them. When you spread out your hands in prayer, I hide my eyes from you; even when you offer many prayers, I am not listening. Your hands are full of blood! Wash and make yourselves clean. Take your evil deeds out of my sight; stop doing wrong. Learn to do right; seek justice. Defend the oppressed. Take up the cause of the fatherless; plead the case of the widow. (Isaiah 1:14–17).

Reflect
Do celebrations of other faiths in your community impact you, and how can you turn those feelings into a positive?

Our day of atonement

Jews submit requests for forgiveness from God on the Day of Atonement. I think we all have to submit requests for forgiveness, not only once a year—on a day when we play and have fun, and then we commit sins for the rest of the year—but every day.

On the occasion of this holiday, I think that we as Christians should ask forgiveness from God and ask forgiveness from those we have sinned against:

- Forgive us for mixing values in our lives. We have become slaves of money, power, and position instead of worshiping God and loving family and friends.
- Forgive us because instead of speaking with tolerance, patience, and humility, we have accused and been impatient with others who don't agree with our doctrine.
- Forgive us for covering the outside of ourselves with false spirituality when the inside of us is suffering from fear and lack of faith.
- Forgive us because we neglected the life of holiness in our daily lives; we have misused the resources God has put in our hands.
- Forgive us for our weak trust in you. We have neglected your calling to be witnesses for you in your land, which is burdened by conflict, anger, and discrimination. Forgive us for not trusting you to take care of us in this land and cultivate thoughts of leaving and emigrating from this land to a more peaceful place.

- Forgive us because we have neglected the call of the Prince of Peace to be peacemakers. Here in Nazareth, we have not actively enough sought reconciliation between our Palestinian people and the Jewish people.

- Forgive us that we have not shown people the living gospel. We have not proclaimed your power, nor have we been a light to the world in your name.

- Forgive us for our selfishness as we measure everything by its benefit to us and not according to your commandments and guidance.

- Forgive us that we run away from the problems of the community in which we live. We only see our own problems and forget the pain of others in our community and our people.

- Forgive us as we live in excess for ourselves and choose not to contribute from the blessings you have endowed upon us, to refugees, orphans, and the poor when they are all around us.

- Forgive us because we do the things you hate such as racism, factionalism, and sexism. Please help us to do as you did, to treat men and women equally.

- Forgive us that we allowed negative ideas and trivial matters to fill our minds instead of everything right and good and positive.

- Forgive us that we only love those who love us. Teach us to love both our neighbor and our enemy, as you commanded us.

- Forgive us because we run toward acknowledgment, positions, and appreciation, and this is precisely contrary to the self-denial that you ask of us.

- Forgive us that we have not put the cross in front of our eyes every day and have neglected the story of the crucifixion of Christ. We haven't reflected on your grace fully enough when we make daily decisions, only remembering you when we go to church again.

Reflect

What are other areas in your life that you should ask forgiveness for?

Set me free from Black Friday

Arabs said in ancient times: "Rebuke is better than flattery." This is true, as we should be more attentive to what is serious and sober than to what is funny, amusing, and imaginary.

The deteriorating conditions of Arabs from the Gulf to North Africa on cultural, scientific, literary, and even humanitarian levels has reversed the old saying. On one side, rebuke has changed to weeping over the past and paying a cost for its tragedies and catastrophes. On the other side, flattery and amusement have prevailed and are now characterized by the consuming flavor that is imported from the West, whether related to goods or culture.

I do not rebuff Western influence itself; we still have a lot to learn from the West as we are already about a light-year behind it. However, it seems that our acceptance of what is happening there is selective and focuses only on consumption matters. I also do not reject the joyful programs that generations of our people have missed for decades because of the conditions of conflict and struggle. We are already fed up with sadness, melancholy, and despair, which are considered almost defining Arab characteristics. Our land deserves life.

One of the latest Western trends that we have adopted is "Black Friday." It is the Friday after Thanksgiving in America—the fourth week of November. It was called "black" because that color refers to the positive balance in contrast to the "red"—which is an indication of the fiscal deficit or negative balance—God forbid! Black Friday inaugurates the shopping season that lasts until Christmas.

There is no doubt that the adoption of an endless-purchase festival on that day in our local markets and the East in general, just like other imported trends, is a sign of globalization; we live in a small world where what happens in one part affects all other parts.

There is no way to write on this subject without mentioning the falsity of the commercial campaigns in our part of the world. It is a reality that most sales are actually untrue, and they mostly depend on "making a fool" of the consumer; this is set in contrast to real discounts in the West.

Because of the crisis of values in which we now seem to live, we have imported "Black Friday," skipping Thanksgiving Day that precedes it, because its essence is unfamiliar and not popular. Unfortunately, true, sincere thanks have become rare and are mostly used for flattery and adulation. Further, we have only adopted the consuming side of the Christmas season, in which the meaning of the birth of the Lord Jesus is lost. The birthday Person stands aside like a stranger, while the people "celebrating" him are distracted with adornments, purchases, and parties. So, too, the meaning of New Year's Day is easily lost—when we are supposed to thank God for the past year, contemplate learned lessons, and plan for the new year.

There is another dimension of the successively adopted events, memorial days, and Western trends; it is a cultural dimension. If we do not pay attention to the Western consumption invasion we will be lost because it has penetrated our culture, our language, our civilization, and our customs. We will lose those distinctive features on the altar of melting in the world's civilization.

We are often amazed by the Western consumption of international quality brands and some cheaply priced goods.

However, we seem to forget that this is only a single face of capitalism. We fail to remember that these products are likely to have been manufactured by the hands of workers in poor, developing countries working without minimum conditions of good work environments or adequate pay.

Shopping in itself—despite the temptation it holds on Black Friday or Boxing Day or during the end-of-season sales—tickles a hidden desire in the hearts of humans that are like a sleeping giant waiting for something to wake him up. It is the desire to own, accumulate, and get more and more. Sometimes, this desire fills a void in the human soul that seeks material things to fill it up. Other times, the extreme desire for consumption meets a person's need to show off what was expensively purchased in front of those who cannot afford it. At other times, we have a desire to buy something at a very low price to be proud of our cleverness, as we managed to seize the opportunity of a discount that others were unaware of.

Thus, if shopping has gone beyond limits, it makes it difficult to develop the qualities that Jesus urged us to have. He asked his disciples to live a life of satisfaction, thanksgiving, fasting, assisting others, and selflessness. Those who are used to living extravagantly by purchasing and shopping beyond their actual need will find it hard to live a life of adequacy and satisfaction.

May God save me from this "Black Friday" and help me focus my eyes on what matters much more—Good Friday.

Reflect

What are some alternatives you can imagine for yourself, rather than participating in Black Friday?

Jesus's diary of a quick visit to Nazareth on Christmas Day

I visited Nazareth in disguise to see how my people were doing on my birthday. A faithful friend lent me his vehicle to reach downtown. I wandered a lot but did not find a place to park. I remembered what my mother had told me about the unavailability of finding a place in Bethlehem for herself, Uncle Joseph, and me, when I was in her womb. Speaking of my mother, Mary, I just imagined how delighted she would be if she accompanied me on this visit today to Nazareth. She loves the place so much and still remembers it; she wishes that its people would love me even more.

I put on shabby clothes and none of my people recognized me. This helped me to see things closely. Despite the cold weather, the town was busy. People were walking in swarming crowds. They looked happy, but I could see that behind their smiling faces there was worry, stress, and anxiety.

On every corner, you could see a decorated green cypress tree that symbolizes hope and life. However, it reminded me of the tree from which they carved the wooden cross. My cross is life eternal; it is the spring of life; there was no need to decorate it. My Father's love for humankind is the real decoration.

I have also seen the children, and adults dressed as Santa Claus. The moment this Santa shows up, everyone is happy. I got to know the reason: he has gifts in his sack. Some people in Nazareth call him the "Sheikh," or Elder, of the season. Why do we need an elder for the season when the Lord of the season is already there— the Christmas Child? Is the generosity of Santa Claus a symbol of all the gifts I offered to humanity on my birthday?

I heard noise and I saw people gathered together in a decorated hall. A distinguished group of public figures were giving speeches, one after another. I listened to their words and I heard bombastic words on peace. I remembered the atmosphere of my birth at Bethlehem where there was no peace. King Herod was chasing us, so my family had to flee, and I became a refugee in Egypt. Then, Herod killed a multitude of children in Bethlehem. I listened further and found that the speakers did not mention my name. Is it the birthday of some other person?

When I went past the houses of the neighborhood where I used to live, I noticed housewives cleaning their houses, cooking, and setting tables with meals for Christmas Eve. The smell of food was mouth-watering; Nazareth women still cook the most delicious food just like they used to do 2,000 years ago. Some people noticed that I was a stranger, but none of them invited me in to dine with them. Maybe my shabby clothes persuaded them to ignore me?

I looked for those who celebrate the season after my own heart. I found some groups in churches singing, praying, and recalling my birth. I found individuals from every denomination and religion giving glory to the Christ child.

I found some others looking for widows, orphans, and sick people to give them a cup of cold water in my name. I was really happy to see them, and I spent a long time with them. They invited me to join in, celebrating the feast together, but I excused myself, saying that we will meet soon at another supper: the wedding supper of the Lamb. Immediately, they recognized me, and then I disappeared.

Reflect

What, in your opinion, would Jesus love if he visited your town on
    Christmas today?

Some aspects of the Incarnation

When you ask a faithful believer and student of the Bible to share the meaning of Advent and Christmas, they seek to link it to the cross. Christ came into the world ultimately to arrive at the Cross for the greatest purpose: the redemption of humanity. This is surely right.

In this sense the meaning of Christmas is linked to another action: the death of Christ on the cross. But does it have a meaning in itself?

I think the most important concept that we often neglect is the Incarnation. God became flesh and dwelt among us, and we have seen his glory, the glory of the one and only Son, who came from the Father, full of grace and truth. What are our lessons in this season of the incarnation of God in the form of a child born in a small town in a poor manger in Bethlehem?

1. The Incarnation is a touch of outreach and love between earth and heaven. The land of misery groans from the horror of sin, which has provoked wars, hatred, and bloodshed. In this time, the hand of God extends to touch the hand of man. He is Emmanuel, God with us. The Creator of the universe visits the earth to find the most beautiful and precious of what his hands have created: human beings.

2. Another aspect of the Incarnation is how it shook the foundations with sound after a long silence. Silence had ruled for more than four hundred years before his birth. One might say that it was the most eloquent silence in history! How or why did God keep silent in his dealings with human beings? He sent his prophets for thousands of years and spoke through them, stating

that his people should return to him. But then he was silent, as if he had despaired. And then the voice of God spoke to us of his Son—the Gospel that the nations had been waiting for. This is the Son of God incarnate!

3. Incarnation is the climax of humility. No one else will ever humble himself like this throughout human history. He who sat on the right hand of the heavenly throne surrendered himself. The one who existed since eternity humbled himself. The one who existed when the earth was founded made himself nothing. He gave himself up to be born in a manger. No one can comprehend the depths of the gap that the Lord has given up in his Incarnation. It is like descending from the Himalaya of the universe to the bottom of the Dead Sea. Isn't he worthy to be followed and to walk in his footsteps of humility?

4. Incarnation is also a real and authentic touch with people. It is the act of God who wears a body and lives among us. He becomes human; he eats and drinks; he is tired and sleeps. He becomes like us and shares our humanity entirely, except in sin. In his Incarnation, he teaches his disciples—you and me—to go to the people, to suffer like them, dream with them, rejoice as one of them.

Reflect

1. Why was there a need for God to be incarnated?
2. What do we mean when we ask missionaries to be immersed in the culture they are serving, and why? How do you think that relates to the Incarnation?

Unlike any other birth

One of the most exciting human experiences is the birth of a baby. The renewal of humanity and its thriving depends on babies being born. It points to the creation of a new life, a whole person with all his or her senses and organs: brain, eyes, skin, and heart.

If the birth of a human being is such an amazing and wonderful matter, how much more amazing is the birth of a child who is a perfect human, and also the perfect God who came to our land?

You would expect the King of Kings to be born in the capital of capitals at that time—in powerful Rome or cultural Athens, but out of his humility he chose the least of Judah's cities. You would have expected the elite of political and religious powers to come and see baby Jesus and present him their gifts, but instead, he received only simple shepherds and Gentile Magi coming from afar.

At the time when all means of comfort and safety are provided for any newborn baby, this unique child, like whom no one has been or would ever be born, did not find a place in any house in Bethlehem and was born in a barn for animals.

We usually congratulate the parents on the birth of their baby, but we should rather congratulate ourselves and all of humanity on the birth of baby Jesus. This was a crucial moment in the history of humankind: God incarnated so we could receive the ultimate blessing.

We often say to new parents, "May the baby be raised enjoying your richness and love," but on this occasion, on the birth of Jesus, we can tell ourselves, *We will be raised enjoying* his *richness and love.*

He became poor so we would be rich. He left the throne in heaven to come to our land as a poor person, so we could be children of the King.

Visitors will give a new mother presents—some are symbolic, like flowers; others are for a celebration, such as chocolate; and some are practical for the baby: clothes, food, diapers, or items for bathing. At the birth of Jesus, the equation was different. Visitors were wondering what they could ever give to the Creator of all things. Even now, you can only offer your heart, stand in awe at his feet, and present gifts that show some aspects of his unique character as the Magi did.

A child's family often prays for his or her growth in good physical, emotional, and mental health; for success; and for walking in the same path of the family. No doubt Christ's family wanted the same for him, but his path would be his own. The words of the Magi, the shepherds, Elder Simeon, and Anna the daughter of Penuel, testified without doubt that this child was sent from God and he was to deliver his people.

The parents of an ordinary child seek to secure a comfortable life for that child, so they devote a special room for him, and they are keen to feed him and take great care of him. In the case of Jesus, things were different, as he had to flee with his parents from the tyranny of Herod and take refuge in Egypt. There is no doubt that God took care of him and used Mary and Joseph to fulfill his needs, but unlike many children that God created, he had to live as a refugee!

People consider the birth of a child a blessed continuation of the human race. They are especially relieved if the child is born after years of infertility. When Jesus was born, he raised an offspring that lasts. That offspring is everyone who believes in his name from every people, nation, and tongue through all ages. He took for himself a people released from the grip of Satan. Hallelujah.

At the birth of such a King—we can do nothing but present the most precious treasures of our humble hearts, surrendering to him and allowing him to lead our lives, resources, and dreams.

Reflect

What are celebrations that people do in your tradition when a baby is born?

Memories of a sheep from Bethlehem

I have always wished I hadn't been born a sheep. The other animals make fun of me because I am fat and I walk slowly. They mock me, whispering that my time has come to be driven to slaughter. I thought that Jacob, the shepherd, loved us and that is why he leads us into green pastures where we eat and eat . . . but now I understand that he is making us fat, so he can earn more money when he sells us.

Several unusual incidents have taken place recently that distracted me from the mockery of other animals and from thinking of my inevitable destiny.

While we were getting warm around the fire in the field of Beit Sahour at night, a strong light burst in the sky, filling the space as if it were daytime. Then, angels appeared and sang in delicate and beautiful voices that made me dance and refreshed my heart along with the hearts of all the flock. Jacob and his friends talked to the angels, but I could not comprehend the words. Even so, I was overwhelmed with much tranquility when I heard them. Then, Jacob hurried, gathered the flock, and returned to town. I was surprised, as we are not used to wandering or walking during late-night hours.

But then, when we got to a barn, Jacob left the rest of the flock outside and accompanied me inside. There, I beheld the face of an infant whose mother had wrapped him in cloths. I had never seen such beauty or delicacy in the face of a child. As for his mom, her compassion prevailed in the barn. I noticed that the baby's father was not there. When he returned, I could sense how kind he was, but I also guessed he was carrying some worries in his heart.

It was very cold in the barn, and as a sign of my love for the baby, I decided to take part in warming him with my breath. I wished I could give my fleece to his mother so she might wrap the baby and warm him.

Jacob and the shepherds talked a lot with the baby's parents. I did not understand what they were saying, but it seemed that the shepherds were telling them with wonder and amazement what they had seen last night in the field.

Their conversation was different from what I was used to hearing, for the shepherds bowed down by the cradle, repeating the same words they had heard the angels say—words about giving glory to God, and about peace and goodwill. I did not hear the baby cry at all during the time I was there. Then, when the shepherds and Jacob were about to leave, Jacob approached me and took me in his arms. I understood that I was to be a gift to this family, and I accepted this with confused emotions, as I was about to depart my friends, though it seemed that I would be with a very special family.

I moved to Bethlehem with this special child and his family, and later, a crowd of men and women came in golden festive garments to visit. I peeped from my position near the baby to see how these people communicated with Mary and Joseph; their language was strange and unintelligible. But I was sure from their gestures that they were talking about a star in the sky. And to my greatest amazement, like the shepherds, they bowed down where the baby was. In the same manner that Jacob handed me as a gift to the family, I saw these rich nobles (maybe even kings) present precious gifts as well! Who could this infant be? He was born in a barn where animals are kept, but angels appear to call his name with the sweetest tunes, and nobles come to bow down and present gifts to him.

I accompanied the family for many weeks. During this period, I saw the calmness of the mother, and I felt that she was keeping in her heart all these wondrous matters that happened to them.

I heard her speak to Joseph (later I understood that he was not her husband but was just her fiancée) about what the old man, Simeon, had told them when they traveled to Jerusalem on the eighth day of the baby's birth. He told her that one day a sword would pierce her soul. I was surprised by Joseph's reply, but it was a turning point in my life. Joseph told her that maybe Simeon meant that this sword is related to what he has understood from the book of Isaiah, that the Son of the Highest will be led like a lamb to the slaughter and as a sheep before its shearers.

I overheard Joseph saying that maybe because this meek infant is the Son of God, Simeon was alerting her that she will suffer because evil ones will lead him to death like a sheep. Mary will be in pain as if a sword has pierced her soul when she sees her son led to death like a sheep.

And many years later, I was delighted to hear the Son of the Highest draw an analogy of himself as a sheep—like me. In fact, he chose to be like a sheep. He did not choose to be like a tiger or a jaguar or any of the other animals. My sorrow that animals were mocking me was then turned into pride and dignity. The Son of the Highest chose to be like me! Even if they lead me to death, I will be like the Son of the Highest, this awesome child in Bethlehem.

Reflect

Why did God choose to be symbolized as a lamb? Can you think of any other images or stories of lambs and sheep in Scripture?

Part Two

The Inner Life

Our courage

D o you know what is common among Martin Luther, Martin Luther King Jr., Yitzhak Rabin, Richard the Lionheart, and Corrie ten Boom? History has considered each of them brave and courageous characters. The first one fought against corruption in the church; the second fought against racial discrimination; the third sought peace; the fourth fought nobly in war; and the last one rebelled against the Nazis' injustices and was able to help persecuted Jews find avenues of escape.

Generally speaking, people admire the brave. The brave in war receive honorary medals, the courageous in breaking the cycle of violence and seeking peace may win the Nobel Peace Prize, and history honors and preserves the memory of those who fought against oppression and tyranny.

When can we describe an action as brave? What distinguishes it from other actions? It is an action that contributes to a supreme human value (such as the freedom of worship, justice, or equality), for which the brave one pays a price or risks his or her life, position, or power. A brave action is sometimes an actual act; at other times, it is the brave refusal to act (such as the rejection of unjust orders that contradict one's principles).

Such a description of courage applies both to men and women of God in the Old Testament. Joseph sacrificed his prestige in the house of Potiphar for the supreme value of *not* sinning against God. Daniel risked his position in the king's palace when he refused to be defiled by the king's food and wine. Elijah opposed Ahab the king and his wicked wife, Jezebel, and worshiped the living God. Nathan the prophet confronted King David with his sin when the latter had used his influence to put Uriah on the front line of a battle so he would be struck down and die, so that David could take Bathsheba, Uriah's wife, as his own. Abigail, the wife of Nabal, risked her life when she went down to David carrying gifts. At that time David was accompanied by hundreds of armed men who were coming to kill her husband, but Abigail was able to persuade David to change his mind.

The New Testament is also rich with courageous figures such as the Virgin Mary, who sacrificed her reputation by accepting the call of God. All of the Marys (the mother of our Lord, the Magdalene, and Mary of Clopas—see John 19:25) who followed the Lord to the cross risked their lives and did not care about the brutality of both the priests and the Romans. Stephen also risked his life to proclaim the truth of the Gospel, and Paul risked his life in Asia Minor to establish churches despite certain persecution.

The one who surpassed them all is the Lord Jesus, who challenged the Roman political system and the religious Jewish regime to convey the principles of the kingdom to everyone and to complete the work of redemption. Jesus also rebuked the Pharisees bravely for their hypocrisy and condemned their hollow faith. He stood valiantly against the temptation of Satan after fasting for forty days and was able to rebuff all his temptations. His entire life on earth was marked by courage; he went against the tide and performed the greatest act of sacrifice and courage of all history to redeem humanity.

Even though we have all of the aforementioned examples of bold faith and God's protection, what could prevent us from standing for the truth courageously? FEAR. The Bible warned us about this:

There is no fear in love. But perfect love drives out fear, because fear has to do with punishment. The one who fears is not made perfect in love. (1 John 4:18)

This means that the lack of love generates fear that in turn prevents courage. The reverse is also true: love removes fear and produces courage.

What kind of love is necessary for courage? It is the love of God and the love of neighbor. My love for God leads me to risk what is precious to me and to stand for truth as God commands me. My love for others makes me willing to take a stand for their wellbeing, even if it entails sacrifice.

Do Christians in your country take a courageous stand for the truth, or are they most often looking for comfort and support, in order to be strong, avoid harm, and keep the status-quo?

Some Christians have taken courageous stances that stand out as bright moments in history, such as the stand against Apartheid in South Africa, for peace and reconciliation in Ireland, and against Nazism in Germany. In contrast, other Christians and churches have stood compliantly with brutal powers, such as those who supported the continuation of slavery in the United States, and the support of the Nazi regime in Europe, or tyrannical communist rule in different parts of the world.

I must keep asking myself, and challenging my church in Nazareth: what will be our response in the Holy Land when we see injustice and brutalization?

Reflect

1. Think of situations where you have displayed courage.

2. What other qualities could prevent a person from taking courageous actions and how do these qualities relate to a lack of love?

3. In your country, what are situations that need a more courageous stance from your church?

Thank you that I am not like other people

Perhaps the strictest of the Lord Jesus's words in the Gospel are those related to the Pharisees and their approach of punctilious adherence to Jewish Law while neglecting the spirit behind that law. Jesus described them as a "brood of vipers," "blind leaders of the blind," and "hypocrites."

The Lord detested the image that the Pharisees portrayed, as they strictly followed the form and overlooked the substance. They clung to the crust and forgot the essence. They were determined to follow the legal technique rather than the legal principle. They lived for self-righteousness and self-glory. They memorized the Law and the meticulous traditions of religion, but they missed the meaning.

The Pharisees considered themselves as God's stewards, controlling the destiny of other people and issuing judgments and criteria that burdened others. Perhaps the ugliest thing they did was condemn others. They adopted exclusion as their approach and issued judgments against others, including Jesus.

Jesus's personal approach was a clear contrast to that of the Pharisees. Jesus followed the principle of grace. When he met Pharisees, the rich, poor, sinners, tax collectors, or lepers, he focused on repairing their core issues, while teaching them how to live with grace. For example, he warned against hatred in the heart, as he saw this as the main cause for murder, and he warned of misplaced sexual desires as he knew they would bring adultery down the road.

Jesus broke the law of doing no work on the Sabbath over and over again in order to do good, especially to heal the sick and to help the miserable. This was in contrast to how the Pharisees lived. Jesus broke the laws that restricted good work and targeted places where he could bless, be merciful, raise, encourage, and give life. Jesus said: "I desire mercy and not sacrifice" (Matthew 9:13).

In our lives today, do we act like the Pharisees? Do we deceive ourselves and set up a similar modern-day system of law adherence that the Lord would detest? Or—sometimes equally dangerous—do we consider ourselves far from the punctilious adherence to the law because we are Christians and our churches believe in grace rather than carrying the burdens of tradition and rituals?

In Luke 18:9–14, the Lord told the parable of the Pharisee and the tax collector. He was speaking to two specific men, the self-righteous Pharisee and the tax collector who humbled himself before God. There are many ways that a modern-day Pharisee of any Christian tradition can imitate the Pharisee of the parable by saying any of the following:

"Thank you, Lord, that I am not a legalist and that my denomination is the best."

"My denomination is the largest and it is the most powerful universal church that represents Christians. Its strength, beauty, and honor fill the universe."

"My denomination is the oldest; it is the origin. All other denominations emerged from it and its teaching and doctrine are the standard and model."

"My church is the most biblical and is traced back to the early church. We are the most active, we have a personal relationship with Christ, and we worship in spirit and truth."

"Thank you, God, that I am from Nazareth, the city of Christ, who was called the Nazarene, and the whole world is turning toward it."

"Thank you, God, that I come from Egypt: the refuge and shelter of the Holy Family from the oppression of Herod."

"Thank you, God, that you have blessed me with an abundance of money and property, and this is certainly because you are pleased with me. I thank you that you did not make me as poor as other people."

Let everyone examine their own heart and let the Lord shake the dust of legalism off us, for Christ's glory.

Reflect

1. What are some prideful phrases used by people to boast in your own country, state, community, or church?
2. Do you see areas in church life that are characterized by legalism? What are they and what can we do about them?

The Divine fingerprint

started by creating light that penetrated darkness. . . . It is my delight to create it since light is one of my characteristics. . . . Yet I was not satisfied.

I saw water everywhere, so I separated it apart upwards and downwards. I was happy with that since water is a symbol of what I am going to give to human beings, that will become in them a spring of water flowing to eternal life. Yet this did not satisfy me.

Beasts, animals, insects, and birds that wander in all the earth, wonderfully I created them. . . . Yet this did not satisfy me.

I created the world so precisely and separated the heavens from the earth, and I was pleased with the work of my hands. . . . Yet this did not satisfy me.

I was determined to create a creature in my image and likeness . . . a creature to have a mutual love relationship with: a being who would share his worries and dreams with me. . . . Not only did I create this being but I also even put my fingerprint in him.

Along with my fingerprint, I knew that my character and traits would pass to him too.

I formed human beings from the dust of the earth and breathed into them my spirit. . . . They are the crown of my creation.

All of my creation will acknowledge their uniqueness since my fingerprint is in them.

I formed them to be able to love, care, and be creative.

I gave them freedom of choice; without this, the enabling love would be meaningless. I will never coerce them to submit to my ways. I will grant them full freedom. After all, this is the essence of what it means to be human. Their freedom is interwoven in their nature—my fingerprint ensures that. However, they chose to disobey despite my warning of the consequences. . . .

They doubted my commandment and were led astray by the serpent to disobedience.

I will not erase them from the earth—as they are the work of my hands.

I created humans beautiful and full of love, yet they ruined my plans with their ill choices, leaving me no option but to let them bear the consequences of their rebellion. Yet, I choose to pay for their sin myself: humans are my creation, and my heart delights in them.

I will enable them to be reborn after I fix the corruption they brought upon themselves.

I will go to the world that I built for them to fill and enjoy. There I will die to pay the wages of their disobedience in trespassing the divine law.

I will redeem them to make them righteous so they will renew their relationship with me. I will regain my glorious nature in them. . . . My divine fingerprint.

Reflect

The Bible does not use the term "fingerprint." What are some biblical parallels to the meaning of that word?

The revival we need

Believers in churches often mention "the glory of God," either in their prayers or sermons or songs. Many say honestly that they as individuals and churches seek the "glory of God" and they wish to be the tool that God uses to reflect God's glory. This term is generally accompanied by roaring emotions that reflect the authenticity of that desire.

But what is the glory of God? What is this thing that we yearn for?

Some believers ask the Lord to show his glory, and by this they mean that they want God to show his strength and majesty in a stormy and powerful revelation as it was with Moses on Sinai, or with Paul when he was caught up to the third heaven. They want the Lord to come with his supernatural power and give them a deep, visible experience. There is no harm in such yearnings, for whoever the Lord touches with his Spirit will inevitably change to become a tool that God will use to fulfill his will. However, we should be aware that our request should not be merely for the supernatural experience.

We should distinguish between asking for "the glory of God" and stating that we are "giving the glory to God." Sometimes believers practice the first and expect the fruits of the second. They will ask for the glory of God in an act of worship and prayer and expect that glory to God in the eyes of non-believers will be obtained. I will explain.

The first is the personal side: giving the glory to God is an individual, personal act. It is simply turning *our* eyes toward God in his goodness, greatness, love, and favor. It is a testimony to God that he is an unchanging, good God. In a time when people are busy giving glory and turning their eyes toward themselves, the focus on God becomes rare. In a time when people reject whatever is not material, it is harder to turn their eyes toward a God that they do not see or touch.

Besides, we may utter words of praise and singing or prayer in our silent time of worship or in parts of other meetings—words where we mention the characteristics of Jesus and thank him for his blessings, favor, and salvation. If we lift those prayers and praises with a true heart, then this will fill the heart of God as well as build the faith of those who hear it. The life of the one who is praying will change and be impacted by drawing nearer to God. And the planting of the principles and values of the kingdom of God on earth, through faithful disciples who make the Lord the master of every aspect of their personal life, brings glory to Jesus too.

The second is the one that reflects that glory on others—what manifests the glory of God and what makes the position of God rise in the eyes of believers and non-believers is a different matter. The mere mentioning of the name of God in praise does not glorify him in the eyes of those who do not believe or those who doubt his goodness or power. The name of God is unmistakably glorified in their eyes only when something extraordinary happens through the work of God in a human being's life. So, when a believer forgives, loves the unlovable, or serves others out of reverence for God, this glorifies the Lord. When a believer excels in a certain field and praises God for their success, then the focus is turned toward God and his name is glorified. There are many examples of the Lord being glorified because a believer chose forgiveness instead of revenge in horrific situations such as murders, wars, massacres, and genocide. The Lord is glorified through the sacrificial life of Mother Teresa and others. Without his work in the life of fallen creation, such good things would not be possible.

The reflection of the glory of God in our lives, in all aspects, is a blessing. God's response to our cry to glorify him holds the revival that we badly need.

Reflect

1. What do you think of when you hear the phrase "seeking the glory of God"?
2. What are other practical ways to seek the glory of God?

Then sings my soul, how great thou art!

T raveling around the world has become accessible to many people due to rising incomes, decreasing airfares, and the increasingly popular culture of entertainment and recreation through travel. This allows people to visit countries close or far and enjoy the nature, culture, facilities, and lifestyle of those places.

It seems impossible that the recreational traveler would not sing and praise God for his incredible creation. The Prophet David sang, "The heavens declare the glory of God; the skies proclaim the work of his hands" (Psalm 19:1). If that was the exclamation by a person who lived in Jerusalem, Bethlehem, and the Judean desert, then someone who travels there from far away should say it even more. How could you visit Switzerland and enjoy the scenery of snow-capped mountains without praising the Creator who painted and designed them? How could you watch Norway's stunning fjords, created with absolute precision, without glorifying their architect? How could you visit South African clean blue waters and yet ignore their Creator? How could you sit down at night in the Naqab desert in southern Israel, look up at the sky, and stare at shining stars, yet continue to ignore the One who creatively perfected them out of nothing? How could you visit the jungles of Brazil and then refer their creation to a coincidence or to absurd cosmic interactions?

Why do we take it for granted that a designer, an inventor, or a builder is there for every device, utility, or house, while we do not do the same with the universe with its composition, details, and design, as if the universe is an orphan that was formed by coincidence?

The person who meditates can easily conclude that a mighty, omnipotent God has designed this universe—including its nature, firmament, and stars. The Creator has made it all accurately and perfectly. The universe is a manifestation of God's supernatural harmony, coordination, balance, beauty, and precision.

All of these are eye-catching manifestations that draw attention to the Creator in nature. However, despite our admiration and excitement for these beauties, they do not provide that continuous joy that fills the human heart. God has designed us so that the only thing that fills the emptiness in our heart is the love of God. Nature's manifestations of God must be followed by a relationship with that loving Creator. The Creator of this beautiful and perfect universe was pleased to take flesh, live in the land of misery, and walk the path of pain to the cross for those he loves. Is a God like this not worth our appreciation, love, and even our devotion?

Reflect

1. Think of three different places that provide you with a vivid sense of the beautiful creation of God.
2. In what way is experiencing God through a relationship with Jesus different from experiencing God through the beauty of nature?

Denying of self—a missing element in modern Christianity

We witness a continual conflict in the Bible between putting forward one's ego on the one hand and acknowledging God's sovereignty and surrendering to him on the other. Adam refused to surrender to God's command not to eat from the fruit of the tree in order to prove to Eve that he was a man of decision, vigor, and choice. Cain rejected God's instructions about the acceptable sacrifice and took another path that he saw good in his eyes—attempting to please God with the fruit of the field. Moses also rejected the teachings of God that prohibited killing, by murdering the Egyptian. David followed his desires and committed adultery with the wife of Uriah. . . . And the list continues.

There is a fierce war between surrender to God and the boastful pride of human beings who promote their power and glory. It is a reflection of the war between the flesh and the spirit.

Jesus urged us:

Whoever wants to be my disciple must deny themselves and take up their cross daily and follow me. (Luke 9:23)

This commandment collides face-to-face especially with the spirit of this generation. For we see the value of the human being, and as a result human freedom and rights, as the basis for everything. Therefore, we call for delegation of authority in all kinds of associations (companies, churches, non-profit organizations, etc.) to increase efficiency. We also call for personal initiatives and startups in the economy to find solutions that seek the welfare of human beings. We call for human development that reinforces the individual and develops their talents and skills. All this leads to empowering human beings and puffing up their ego. If these attempts bring fruit, then that person excels, advances, and succeeds, and thus their arrogance increases and their ego aspires to even more personal success.

How does this reconcile with the Lord's commandment to his followers to deny themselves and take up their cross? How will you deny yourself when you are overflowing with self-confidence, empowerment, enabling, and reinforcement?

Some think that self-denial means sheltering, asceticism, and living like a monk. Some see it as a refuge for helplessness, regressing, and failure. However, it is neither. It is a oneness in the divine entity. It is being crucified with Christ, so that he lives in us (Galatians 2:20).

Unfortunately, when we impose our will on God, God does not live in us, but rather we seek to "live in him," so to speak. We put our agendas and our thoughts in the center, and we refer them to God. We color our attitude as one of God's making and will, when he is truly absent from it.

God has left the struggle between the dominion of self and the denial of self to our choice. He has not imposed the outcome on us. However, some Christians are ashamed of their choice reflected in preferring their personal agenda, viewing their own glory over carrying the cross for Christ. Therefore, they will not proclaim Christ's crushing victory by carrying their cross.

The uncovering of the fake self that has "put on" divine clothes but is actually individualistic and concerned only about itself does not happen generally through a supernatural encounter with God. Instead, this happens through real humility before people (and that is a true reflection of self-denial and surrender of God's will), and acceptance of accountability and submission to authorities. The examination of its authenticity is through self-testing, confession of wrong, and repentance. The individual spirit that does not accept criticism or the contribution of the other in teamwork, but is characterized by loneliness and dictatorship, and claims exclusive knowledge of God's will and revelations, has not denied itself. It imposes itself and its will on the will of God, away from his purpose, so that the opposite happens.

The discernment of self-denial will occur in small daily things.

So, if we will be faithful with the little daily matters in order to live in self-denial, God will put us in charge of many things, for the glory of his name.

Reflect

1. What does the rejection of denying one's self create in the church?

2. How does the existence of self-denying believers in churches have an impact on nonbelievers who observe the church?

Between yesterday's kingdom and tomorrow's

My friend Dr. Bryson Arthur recently said that Christians are divided into two categories: those who are attached to the past kingdom of Jesus, and those who set their eyes on the future kingdom of Jesus. The former are immersed in the details of Jesus's life on earth, and they often overlook the fact that Jesus is coming again and that it is necessary to be vigilant to receive him back. The latter focus their attention on the return of the Lord to our world, and so they study the prophecies and look for signs of his fast-approaching coming, and as a result, they often neglect his life and teachings on earth.

Both the kingdom of the past and the kingdom of the future are well expressed in the Lord's Supper:

Do this . . . in remembrance of me . . . you proclaim the Lord's death until he comes. (1 Corinthians 11:25, 26)

I wonder where Christians in the Holy Land stand between these two types, and to which one does our heart cling if indeed it clings at all to anything? I also wonder about the influence of these two categories on the present kingdom of God.

The Lord has given us the honor to live on the land where he lived, where his prophets had lived before him, and where his disciples have lived after him. This fact connects us not only spiritually to Christ through his book and our relationship with him but also geographically through seeing the places that witnessed Christ's doings among humans.

For those of us who live here, we can easily imagine Jesus as a child playing with his friends around the area of Mary's well in

Nazareth, on the same piece of land where the Baptist School I lead is located today. He plays while his mother is conversing with the women of the town around the spring. What kind of play is it with a sinless, omniscient, eternal child?

We can imagine Jesus sitting with his mother calmly at the wedding in Cana—Cana is a mere six kilometers from Nazareth—before they ran out of wine at the house. Was the wedding in the area of Church Street and the house of Abu Ibrahim today or was it at the area where Adel's Salon is? Maybe it was where Cana Wedding Chapel (my grandparents' home) now is. Cana—the land of pomegranates, cafes, and chronic heavy traffic, today—once received the young man who turned water into wine.

For Arab Christians living in the Holy Land, our geographical proximity and our belonging to the land add another dimension to our Christian faith. It is a mistake to depend on this advantage rather than on an intimate personal relationship with the Lord or on the study of his Word, but ignoring this dimension also makes one lose a beautiful grace from the kingdom of the past.

However, our attachment to the kingdom of the future motivates us to wait for the second coming of the Lord and to look for that day when we will be with him forever. It motivates us to keep this in our perpetual consciousness so that we may have the mentality of the one whose vessel is filled with oil waiting for the bridegroom. Before Jesus's first coming, dozens of verses prophesied his coming with details about his birth, ministry, death, and resurrection, and they were all fulfilled. Similarly, the faithfulness of the Lord is sure and non-negotiable; he will come again, and the prophecies concerning the future will also be fulfilled. Do we neglect the coming kingdom? As Christians living in his land, with the eyes of faith we have witnessed the evidence of his first coming, and we should believe the fact of his second coming. With the eyes of faith, we see Jesus establishing the kingdom of the future, where justice and peace reign, and we will live there joyously with our Redeemer.

The commemoration of the past kingdom and the anticipation of the future kingdom must both work together and be poured into the present kingdom of Christ in our lives on this very earth in our country. And the anticipation of the future kingdom, after the return of the Lord, leads us to a life of spiritual vigilance and awakening. It is the life of active believers who are redeeming the time because they are aware that the Lord is near and at the door.

Reflect

1. Where do you place yourself on the scale between those connected to the past kingdom of Jesus and those who are connected to his future kingdom?
2. How would your life of faith be different if you balanced attention to both "kingdoms"?

The work of the Great Physician

The medical doctor's profession has returned to be the dream of every Arab mother for her son (and sometimes her daughter) in my country. As research progresses, the level of medical service and the standard of living increase, the average age has been increasing, accompanied by numerous medical problems and, consequently, an increasing demand for doctors.

Therefore, the profession of medicine has become more attractive than in the past, as its job is guaranteed and its salary is more than reasonable, and it is reachable even for Arabs in Israel, although it requires long hours and many years of study and specialization.

The fact that a doctor has the possible solution for patients at a time when we are more obsessed with our comfort and health than ever before in history, raises the status of the medical profession, too. It is a ministry of healing to humans in one of their most difficult moments.

The Lord embodied this profession and the mission behind it as he did other professions. He is an engineer, a lawyer, a shepherd, and also . . . a doctor. Jesus embodied in his life a skilled doctor who does not disappoint. He embodied this in different ways:

He is the anesthesiologist who was brilliant in his work when he put Adam to deep sleep before conducting the operation that took a rib to create Eve (Genesis 2:21).

He is also a brilliant surgeon who completed the process of carefully taking the rib from Adam.

He is the distinguished dermatologist who cured Naaman the Syrian from his leprosy without leaving any trace, and likewise in healing the ten lepers in the New Testament (Luke 17:12; see also Matthew 8:1–5).

Jesus is the best hematologist, for he stopped the continuous hemorrhage of the bleeding woman (Matthew 9:20). He is the most brilliant surgeon as he reconnected the ear of the high priest's servant Malchus (John 18:10).

He is the best ophthalmologist, for he opened the eyes of the one born blind (John 9:32) and the two blind men on the way to Jericho (Matthew 9:27). The Great Doctor did not need tests and complicated procedures to improve their vision, but he returned their eyesight completely to what I presume was 20/20, if not better.

Jesus also cured the paraplegic that his friends lowered from the ceiling, proving that he was not only the best orthopedic doctor but a neurologist and an excellent general practitioner. Bringing the bones back to life in a paraplegic requires various aspects of the medical disciplines (Matthew 9).

He also healed his apostle Peter's mother-in-law, who had a fever (Matthew 8:15–16). He is also the psychologist who turns the psychologically troubled into psychologically well people, as he did with the two men in the region of the Gadarenes (Matthew 8:28).

After all, God created us, and therefore he has the knowledge and the understanding of every rib, bone, blood vessel, artery, cartilage, and even cell.

He is a general practitioner who is completely proficient in all the known and unknown medical disciplines. He does not need the patient telling him what his symptoms are and what his medical history includes, for he is the examiner of hearts and knows everything. He also does not require imaging and tests to diagnose the disease. He does not require blood tests, neither does he need X-Rays or CT scans or Ultrasound or MRI machines. He diagnoses and heals immediately.

Jesus the Great Doctor heals with mercy and kindness. Glory to God!

Reflect

Jesus was also called "teacher." In what ways and areas does Jesus exemplify "teacher"?

The effect of distorted thoughts on worshipers

The process of worshiping the Lord is a process that requires activation of the mind. Christ demanded that we love God (the broad concept of worship) with all our mind, and Paul called it our "reasonable service" (Romans 12:1b KJV).

In the process of worship, intentionally or unintentionally the worshiper has a mental picture of Christ, who might be doing a great thing in their life, and thus they are grateful and their appreciation for Christ increases. The worshiper might also have a mental picture of Christ on the cross or during his resurrection, or maybe of his being compassionate with children, or his conversation with the Samaritan woman, or any other image that the Bible provides us with for Christ. Of course, the human mind is more complex and far more sophisticated than the greatest computer. Hence, the mental image about God in the mind is associated with the teaching one hears. That image might be similar to that told by a priest or a pastor. It may be mixed up with pictures in films that one has watched, or visualizations of what it is like reading the Bible or even in coloring books for children about Jesus's life. (Sunday school sticks with many of us!)

Because of the vast flow of information from the internet and social media and what the worshiper reads and hears, the image is sometimes distorted. There have been many who claim to be followers of Christ, even though Christ may be disassociated from them. For example, a ruthless capitalist who persecutes and neglects the poor might attribute their orientation to Christianity (because of the principle of personal responsibility). Or a socialist who wants to rob the rich in the name of mercy might claim to represent Christ who made all people equal. The father who is cruel to his children in the name of bringing them up "right" might cite the Bible to defend his actions. The mother who spoils her children might justify this by the principle of mercy in the Bible.

This idea is not confined to humans who act selectively by following a partial application of a biblical principle, neglecting closely attached and complementary principles. Some people go even further by distorting the image of Jesus, describing him as merely a Jewish teacher of the Torah. Another group describes him as a Palestinian militant for liberation, or as a homeless liberal, or a fanatical legalist.

All these images, analogies, and interpretations distort the mind of the worshiper, not to mention the sin that strikes worship at the core and causes an imbalance of values and concepts. This consequently leads to confusion and contaminates the purity necessary for worship, moving us away from the renewed mind (Romans 12:2), and we remain with an old mind that gathers ideas, opinions, and images from any source.

How then could you save your mind and your thoughts? How can you separate the wheat from the chaff? How can you expel the defiled and deformed and keep the pure and true? How can you replace old, contaminated concepts and replace them with new, sound perceptions?

Professor Muna Maroun has led a team of researchers at the University of Haifa's Department of Neurobiology. They have worked together to erase some painful human memories, such as those imprinted on the mind after traumas such as accidents, rape, or physical abuse. Perhaps we need tools that combine neuroscience and spirituality to do similar deletions of information and mental images that distort our concept of Christ.

I am not an expert in neuroscience and brain science, but my spiritual experience leads me to the notion that what drives away distorted and imaginary memories are bright, clean, and real thoughts. The light shines in the darkness (John 1:5), and streams of water sweep away the dirt. Thus, when the darkness dissipates or the dirt disappears, the clean air in the lit space can be a seedbed of worship (2 Corinthians 10:5).

When the written or spoken words of the Bible enter, the words of distortion and falsification are cast out. When church music or tones that evoke feelings of beauty and nobility are heard, bustling and noise are silenced. We allow love to touch us if we touch others by love. Then, feelings of anger, bitterness, and hatred depart.

Thus, the apostle Paul said:

Finally, brothers and sisters, whatever is true, whatever is noble, whatever is right, whatever is pure, whatever is lovely, whatever is admirable—if anything is excellent or praiseworthy—think about such things. (Philippians 4:8)

Reflect
Think of three practical ways you can "clean" your thoughts before worship.

Evangelical and proud

Dear brother and sister,

Grace and mercy in the name of Jesus, the Redeemer!

You have considered me a heretic, although I am a Christian just like you. You have considered Evangelicals as outsiders to Christianity, although they follow the Word of God in the Bible without adding or taking away.

Christianity is like a mosaic made of multicolored pieces of different sizes and shapes. Evangelicals (sometimes called Bible churches, or Reformed Churches, independent churches, or people in some of the "mainline" denominations that identify themselves, too, by the name) are a beautiful and brilliant piece in this mosaic.

I am proud to be an Evangelical, since Evangelicals take their Christian faith seriously and have always prioritized the personal relationship between humankind and Jesus.

Being described as "Evangelical" entails that we are "bearers of good news" and that we take our name seriously and take seriously the commission of the Lord Jesus, before his ascension to heaven, to preach the gospel to every creature. It goes beyond just preaching the good news to serving physical needs in hospitals and schools as well as social justice matters all around the world.

Let me kindly draw your attention to the fact that Evangelicals today are the most active and growing Christian groups in the whole world. At a time when Christian missionary work in Europe and North America is generally receding, the missionary work of Evangelicals around the world (in India, China, Brazil, the

Philippines, Nigeria, and many others) is flourishing and growing stronger, and millions are accepting Jesus.

See the history books, my friends, and you will also find that we are the spiritual sons and daughters of heroes of the faith such as William Wilberforce, Corrie ten Boom, Joni Eareckson Tada, and Dietrich Bonhoeffer. Many of the early Evangelicals in Europe paid a heavy price for their faith and had to flee, losing their possessions and even dying for their right to worship as they believed.

Many people have also had to flee to North America to escape persecution because of their beliefs. Therefore, do not consider us laggards or leisured and pampered people; we are seeking to be worthy of being called by the name "Evangelicals," for which we paid dearly with the blood of martyrs.

We are not churches of new fashion trends and crazes, but we are an expansion of the early church of the Book of Acts.

The disciples and the early believers worshiped God in homes, and when the persecution intensified they fled to the mountains and gathered in caves. They worshiped the Lord simply by singing and reading from the word of the Lord and listening to preaching. There have been groups that have been doing so throughout the ages since the Day of Pentecost. We follow this same approach.

Evangelical churches are flexible and dynamic, and we can easily adapt ourselves to the community's needs because we do not follow a complex system. A local church is free to easily do what the Lord guides it to do. Every member of the church is valued. We all share with others in trying to find the path that the Lord has prepared. This is in addition to our responsibility to contribute to the implementation of God's declared will.

I hear you mock us because we are not what you call a "unified church," but different churches with multiple names. Our diversity should not be considered disgraceful. The Lord has established our multiple churches charmingly; each church tends to innovate and become specialized in an aspect; yet we all celebrate and enjoy the creativity of the other.

We see Baptist Evangelicals often excelling in evangelism, Nazarene Evangelicals in Sunday school programs, Pentecostal Evangelicals in worship and praise, and Brethren Evangelicals in the study of the Word of God in depth and detail. We do respect pluralism in unity.

We all love the Lord and his Word, which we hold above all considerations. We seek the love of God and the love of our neighbor just as the Lord called us. Please know, my friend, that whatever you claim against us, I am Evangelical and proud of it.

With the love of Christ,
Botrus

Reflect
What are special elements of church life in your church that you
    mention when someone begins to criticize?

Part Three

Challenges to Faith

An indifferent intellectual

Many Arab Christian intellectuals boast that they do not care about faith (or "religion"—a term that some prefer to use, but I will not discuss the difference between the terms here). I want to focus on a sub-group: those who are ignorant about all the matters of their Christian faith. These are people who are being sincere when they say they are unaware of their religion's affairs and details. Despite their education and knowledge in different fields, this group deliberately avoids details in matters of faith. For them, religion is the cause of divisions and conflicts among people.

Since Christians are a minority in our society, here in Israel and the Middle East some believe that denying the Christian faith or at least being ignorant about its essence is one of their contributions to unity. They desire that people of other religions also disavow theirs so that we can all gather based on a common non-religious culture and thus live together in harmony.

I believe that this indifferent approach to religion, which I see in many who call themselves intellectuals, is based on two grave mistakes.

First, a person cannot be knowledgeable about everything in life. This is because life is infinite and the information regarding it is also endless. Educated persons of the twenty-first century are characterized by curiosity; they ask a lot of questions and care about the different affairs of life. They are familiar with politics, sociology, economics, and various civilizations. They are good readers and are attentive to news happening across the world. Educated persons are well-informed on many subjects.

Do we describe a person who is informed only about celebrity news and athletes, for example, as an intellectual person? I think the answer is no. This is because we expect the intellectual to be knowledgeable about more important and crucial things than just music and sports. An intellectual should be interested in the fundamental affairs of life.

Different religions claim that there is life after death. The duration of human life on earth is typically seventy or eighty years, whereas what these religions consider to be the real life are the endless years after death. Is neglecting a subject of such utmost importance, and being unaware of its details, right for a person who claims to be an intellectual?

Second, their faulty approach relates to the extent of its success and applicability on the ground. Religion is a very important element of the identity of every human being and cannot be forcefully removed from the components of one's personality. The exclusion of religious elements from our identity to please others, as these intellectuals have done, does not earn us respect, especially in Middle Eastern society. The disavowal of the Christian faith or even the lack of knowledge about it has not previously led to the formation of a non-religious segment of people from different faiths. It has not led to establishing a segment that is tolerant and whose relationship to each other is not blemished by their dissimilar creeds. Christian Arabs are indeed almost the only ones who have taken this denying attitude toward their religion, while intellectuals of other faiths have not relinquished the legacy of their parents' and grandparents' tradition.

It is incumbent upon true intellectuals to take religion, any religion, seriously and examine its credibility. Careful knowledge will inevitably lead to a crucial life decision.

Reflect

1. Can you think of other areas of which if people are unaware, then they strip themselves of being "intellectuals"?

2. What are the areas you feel you are not knowledgeable about?

You've turned your back on God; don't be surprised by the result

In many public gatherings today one can often hear complaints about people's conduct, especially the behavior of young men. They lament a bygone era and lost morals. Perhaps this nostalgia carries some falsification of reality and exaggeration in portraying the past as bright and shiny while the present is seen as dark and gloomy. However, complaining and discontentment have a foundation in society's core that is recognized by the near, the far, and everyone who has witnessed the change in public morals over the years. Everyone yearns for kind people, mutual good treatment of neighbors, fraternity among people of different traditions and faiths, courtesy to the elderly, security in the streets, and other peace-filled qualities of a good society.

Evidence of this massive change can be traced through hard data, such as divorce and crime rates, court cases, disputes between siblings, neighbors, and so on. Municipalities, police, schools, and community-based organizations hold seminars to discuss these phenomena, especially violence. Community leaders, social workers, and police officers express their opinions and present suggestions to deal with this plague—as many like to call it.

We find that one person proposes to intensify discipline in schools while another emphasizes the importance of upbringing at home. A third suggests that the police should strike with an iron fist to enhance their authority, deterrence, and effectiveness. A fourth recommends that the Friday sermon at the mosque and the Sunday sermon at the church should be a platform to alert people about violence, its harm, and its opposition to the "heavenly" messages. There are so many more suggestions among concerned citizens.

These suggestions are good, and if initiatives have been joined and powers have been united, our society will change for the better, but I think that all those interested are missing an important fact.

Christians' attainment of advanced academic degrees in our society has been accompanied by an increasing trend of atheism and alienation from the Church and the Bible. Some believe that enlightenment and openness are contrary to faith and so they put faith aside. For many, religion has become a sign of backwardness, but this is a grave error. The inevitable results are broken cisterns that can hold no water because their theories exclude the Lord. Those who believe these theories think that by their strength they can shape a better society, but the result, as we have seen, is the exact opposite.

How can violence be stopped without moral values? How do you require people to be kind and polite in dealing with others without a higher standard to aspire to? How do we ask for honesty at work while there is no example to follow?

Without God, the standard, the model, and the value will be lost: we labor in vain, our efforts are futile, and we cannot strive higher than his theories and principles because there is no motivation. There are no morals without set values and no set values without a commissioner of values who surpasses us and sets for us a standard of life.

Different movements have tried to create an alternative to life in the hands of the Lord and to the level he set for us, but they have all failed miserably. They have declared that God is dead and brazenly set themselves up as his successors. The personal life of the leaders of these movements have been characterized by adultery, bloodiness, and thuggery. The results of their work and theories have plagued the world's population. The twentieth century was the bloodiest century since the dawn of humankind.

Without God, there is no deterrent. What could prevent humans from killing each other and what deters them from plundering each other's possessions if fear of accountability or love of a generous Creator is absent? Why do I obey a human theory (even if it is valid in some respects) when it has been developed by humans like you and me?

Without a divine criterion of good values in which we believe and to which we strive to act, violence will not be alleviated. Without a pure model that calls for love and applies it just like the Lord Jesus, people will not reconcile with each other. Without a divine book that includes high principles, our lives will never be uplifting.

The nostalgia for a safe past characterized by kindness, love, coexistence, and peace could never be reached by wishing, but rather by a return to divine values that include God and consequently turn fruitful.

Reflect

How do we reconcile the thesis of this article with the fact that some of the safest countries are secular-atheist countries and some of the most violent are religious ones?

How dare you be an atheist!

These days a growing number of people, especially youth, are proclaiming in public that they are atheists.

I do not oppose the personal freedom of every human being to believe whatever they want, to declare it publicly, and even to call others to follow. Believing in God, just like disbelief in God, is a choice, a privilege, and a right for each human being to adopt.

I believe that the ability and the freedom to choose is part of our internal being, as we are created after the image of God. There is a difference between forcing someone to believe in something and their voluntarily believing in it. Faith indicates that you are personally convinced of what you believe, and so forcing you to believe it makes the whole thing absurd and senseless.

However, I wonder how those "atheists" speak lightly and declare their convictions so easily. To ask whether God exists or not is a very tough and thorny question, and the outcome of the answer is even more complicated. My intention is not to discuss the different approaches that religions adopt on the means to reach God and satisfy him, or the way that each religion has set regarding the path that human beings must follow.

Basically and simply, I want to rely on the wager introduced by the French scientist Blaise Pascal and rephrase what he said as follows: if God exists and a person lived their life believing in God's existence, then they are safe and they will obtain eternal life after death. All that they have supposedly lost are the years they have spent on earth trying to satisfy God—if we could ever call it a loss. However, if they rejected the existence of God and at the end of their life, they found out that God exists, then they will have lost their eternal life and they will have only won living their years on earth as they liked—if we ever called this winning. So we can either live a life that is spent trying to please God and gain eternal life with God or live a life trying to please ourselves and spend our eternity without God.

Truly understanding the potential profit and loss in this existential bet leads us to the conclusion that it is better and more profitable to believe in the presence of God—even if it is merely from the perspective of profit and loss. The comparison between the profit gained from an immeasurable eternal life and the gains of life on earth—from 70 to 80 years at most—leads us to the result that even if the probability of God's existence is small (and I do not claim this), it will always be better and safer to believe in God!

Even if atheists regard this bet of profit and loss calculation as a failure, I am surprised by their confident decision that there is no God. The existence of the universe in its complexity and accuracy suggests at first sight that at least there is a Creator. Therefore, if logic only is implemented, the belief that there is no such Creator should not be decided that quickly, easily, and recklessly. It requires strong and accumulated evidence as the bet is tough, and in my opinion, is not in favor of the atheist.

However, it seems that gathering such accumulated evidence to make such a fateful decision is difficult and troublesome, so I am surprised at the claim of the absence of God. Despite great scientific development, humans still feel our way very slowly and never come close to exploring the secrets of the universe in astronomy, biology, chemistry, and physics. Pioneer groups of heroic scientists and researchers funded by billions of dollars to do research and make discoveries rejoice and cheer when they discover something new in any scientific field. They rejoice when they discover new things even if they have not yet come close to understanding either their own essence or the possibility of reconstructing themselves, or even imagining how they were created!

Hence, how does the person who has just dipped once into this vast ocean of science dare to claim that they know the origin of the universe and decide on it, especially seeing that the question has its existential consequences? Such a belief in the absence of God requires strong and powerful evidence (it should be decided after studying science and philosophy and looking into contradictory arguments and grasping them) rather than denying God recklessly and carelessly as many do!

I recommend some humility before uttering definitive statements regarding God's existence or non-existence!

Reflect

1. Why is a declaration of atheism considered a large risk?
2. Why, in your opinion, do many young people find it easy to declare that they do not believe that God exists?

The "enlightenment" of some, and their ignorance of what's crucial

One way that minorities seek to distinguish themselves among the majority with whom they live is by excelling in science, professional occupations, or even criminality. The best example of this is perhaps the Jewish people, who have distinguished themselves as a minority for centuries in both West and East. They have excelled in science, literature, communication, and commerce, and they have occupied sensitive places in the countries where they have lived, despite their small numbers. Another example is the Armenian people, who have distinguished themselves in the East in many areas of professional craftsmanship, including photography, bookbinding, and other areas.

Arab Christians in the Middle East are a minority among Muslims and Jews in Israel. We follow the path of science and education, seeking excellence. Political power is out of our hands because we are a minority, and we lack the power of these larger groups, so we often resort to science and study.

Indeed, Arab Christians represent the highest percentage of the educated among certain segments of society in Israel, where every home of Arab Christians embraces at least one university graduate. We proudly say that Arab Christians in Israel (and in the rest of the countries of the Middle East) receive advanced academic degrees and seek to study even if it means traveling to the ends of the earth. Families of low, average, and above average income alike use all their energy and savings to ensure a good education for their sons and daughters. For many, a university degree is not only an economic guarantee but also a passport in case of turbulence in our troubled part of the world. In case of trouble, a university degree will become a guarantee for the displaced to work and succeed in another country of their chosen destination.

This academic education is usually coupled with broad cultural knowledge and a wide range of information on different subjects. Arab Christians, in other words, seem often to become "intellectuals."

Many of our intellectuals are familiar with domestic and regional politics and are well acquainted with Marxism, imperialism, and nationalism. Our Arab Christian intellectuals are aware of issues of economy and consumption and are familiar with the names of singers, artists, and actors—both Arab and foreign. Arab Christians here are also characterized by their love of traveling and tourism; they visit different countries of the world, gaining experience and knowledge about the cultures of the world.

What's incongruous is how the Arab Christian intellectual's knowledge often seems to come to an end when it concerns the knowledge of the Bible and Christianity.

Suddenly, you find that the Christian intellectual, who is familiar with the affairs of life, is ignorant. It is funny but sad to hear them say that Jesus Christ permitted drinking wine when they cite "wine gladdens human hearts" (they attribute this part of the verse from Psalm 104:15a to Jesus although he never uttered it). At other times, you hear them say that all religions call for the same thing, or that religions are reducible to moral laws. Worst of all, you hear those who bear the name of Christ and claim to be intellectuals say that Christianity calls for salvation by good deeds. What a misinformed pearl of wisdom this is by those who have not even read the Bible and have not devoted time to studying matters of faith. Ignorance is widespread. Many people do not know that the "Latin" Church is the same as the Catholic Church, and its center is in the Vatican. Others do not distinguish between Martin Luther and Martin Luther King Jr. A few only know the reasons for the division between the Eastern and Western Churches, and these are just a few examples of the ignorance.

Some educated Christians who are ignorant of their religion are exaggerating when they show pride in their ignorance and profess that they do not attend church or pay attention to religion. Many would do so simply to integrate into the Muslim majority and to portray themselves as non-fanatical secularists, although Christian faith and knowledge does not at all mean intolerance. Knowing our Christian faith is part of our Arab Christian identity. Our Christianity did not begin out of nowhere; it started from the work of the Lord Jesus through the Cross and the Resurrection, the early church we read about in the book of Acts, and long years of the spread of Christianity. Hence, we should know our faith— even if only for the purpose of being educated and informed.

Even if we think that such knowledge is unimportant, Christianity and the Bible have already had a greater impact on the world than any other movement or idea in history. The Christian faith began in the Middle East, is the foundation of European, African, and American communities, and has had a long-lasting influence on the whole world. It is, therefore, necessary for those interested in the human experience who consider themselves citizens of the world to know about it.

What is more important is that the Bible contains not only the most noble of teachings, even according to non-Christians, but it contains what Jesus taught about choosing the right path in the present life and about reaching the future life. One of the characteristics of an intellectual is knowing how to distinguish the wheat from the chaff; hence, one who claims to be an intellectual must read carefully what the Bible says about the meaning of life and the way of salvation, since these are the most important questions in life.

Reflect

1. What do you think "enlightenment" means?
2. How can we determine if something is crucial for our understanding?

Be careful what you believe

had a conversation with a teacher of Christian religion at one of Israel's schools. I asked him how his students perceive God. He replied that the overwhelming majority believe in God, while only a few speak of atheism. However, those who believe in God have invented a god of their own with special qualities; it is a god made up in their minds. This god is far away from them and does not deserve to be contacted or prayed to. He is also not worthy of sharing their daily lives. Or, their god is only a god of mercy who knows no justice and does not care about sin. He does not and will not condemn anyone. In their god creations, all religions share the same deity and the way to salvation is similar; all roads lead to heaven. They have not only created imaginary gods, but they have also placed the true God on the altar of compromise with believers of other religions.

It seems that even many Christians in our country share these opinions. They believe in an entity called "God," but what they attribute to him does not match in any way what he has announced about himself in the Bible. A sense of relationship with this God has gone missing, and God no longer has an impact on their lives. He is not the God of the Bible who enjoys supreme power and who showed his redemptive love on the Cross. He is a god of their invention fashioned according to their whims, so he turns out to be a puppet, small and far away.

This perception of God is misguided and is one of the most dangerous evil plots, as the outcome will be that those who believe it will mistakenly think they are righteous. They consider themselves believers in God, trying to do good, and perhaps even thinking they enjoy "better" morals than other human beings. In this way, they think they do not need to hear about the true God: the God of the New Testament.

The Lord commanded his disciples in every age and time to fulfill the Great Commission: to go to all the world and make disciples (see Matthew 28:16–20). However, we believe in the teaching of the New Testament that human beings are saved and become disciples if they trust in Jesus, believe in his propitiatory work on the cross, and live by this faith in relationship with the Lord. The Great Commission contradicts and is opposite to the aforementioned satanic misguidance that tarnishes the conscience of the person who has come to believe that they do not need the true God.

Many of those who claim these "new" and erroneous understandings of God say that they have come to their conclusions using scientific and logical methodologies. But logic and scientific thinking calls for examining facts, and they usually have not taken the time to examine the identity of the God of Christians in the light of what God says about himself, and what history says about him. They need to examine his qualities and his message, but they have fallen into the trap of faith in a God that does not exist; their god is simply the product of their imaginations.

There are many apologetic books of Christian faith—by C. S. Lewis, Timothy Keller, William Lane Craig, Josh McDowell, and others—that discuss the subjects of religion and faith in a professional and logical way, proving that Christian faith according to the Bible deserves to be taken seriously.

But unfortunately, many who were entrusted with the message of the Gospel are in a deep sleep, and so they have not confronted others who claim made-up gods. They are like dead fish that are swept away by the current. Instead of confirming the foundations of faith received from the Scriptures and the saints, they are caught in the trap of the social gospel, or sermons on good manners, or issues of war and peace, or an almost exclusive focus on the environment. These are important subjects, but they should originate from the foundations of correct doctrine.

We should address this grave misguidance at the heart because it leads people to perdition. Whoever believes in a god who is different from the one we were evangelized to follow, shall be cursed and destined to follow the god they have invented until it leads them to the bottomless pit. There is no alternative other than attacking this way of thinking so that we cast down arguments against the knowledge of Christ.

Reflect

1. What is the deluding idea that the author is referring to?
2. Why do you think some people won't deal with the question of their Savior with the same scientific methodology that they use elsewhere?

University campuses and vanity of vanities

In my childhood forty years ago I remember that those who could complete their undergraduate study were few, holders of a post-graduate degree were even fewer, and holders of a doctorate in any branch other than medicine were almost nonexistent.

The last part of the twentieth century witnessed a dramatic increase in the access of people to higher education. Completing undergraduate study in the universities of Israel and abroad has become normal and common: tens of thousands of Arabs enroll in postgraduate study programs, and a few thousand pursue doctoral programs every year. This flood of university degrees is accompanied by greater professional qualifications, social and scientific progress, and a higher standard of living. It is also accompanied by public literacy and greater knowledge about what is going on in the world.

Is the picture rosy in all its aspects? What is the impact of this on the church? Western-influenced educational curricula dominate in Israeli universities, often challenging the conservative views that Christian Arab students start with when they begin their university study.

Students of biology learn about evolution as if it were an indisputable undeniable fact when it is still a theory. The university student who studies English literature is being taught that the Christian influence on Western literature is just like the influence of Sophocles's legends. The one who studies philosophy is being confronted with the theories of Frederick Nietzsche, Jean-Paul Sartre, and Existentialism, which all oppose Christianity. This means that the student does not find someone who presents the Christian view that stands against the theories of atheists.

Christian Arab students attend university with anticipation and fear as they are still of a tender age. They are studying in Hebrew, their second or even third language. They desire to be accepted and want to learn the academic material as it is so that they may pass the exam. Even if they want to argue or discuss, they are generally not well prepared to develop critical ideas for what they hear in the lecture halls or read in books. Because of this, they have an even more difficult time speaking out about such issues. The negative impact on these students is not limited only to education curricula, but extends to the hormone-driven environment of young people, especially when they are away from parental supervision. Usually, the minority seeks to imitate the majority, and so Arabs seek to imitate the Jews (or the Europeans, or the Americans), and leave behind a conservative lifestyle that they likely learned from their family of origin.

The students are then deeply perplexed; their whole being, their values, and their faith are shaken; many Christian students forsake their belief during this period of their lives. To find justification for abandoning it, they use words like education, enlightenment, and openness. Undoubtedly, the results are dire, and many young university graduates return to their cities and villages holding high university degrees, but holding a low view of their faith. They have filled their minds with information and theories but emptied their souls of values and faith.

This is not a warning against learning. Such a choice will cause the Christian community to be even more marginalized and lose any influence on our society, which is continuously undergoing scientific and economic development. It is an encouragement for

Christians to hold fast to our saving faith even while being amid non-Christian communities or values.

It is crucial to emphasize that the Christian faith is suitable both for the simple, uneducated person and for the holder of high academic degrees who can find in the theology of our faith whatever their hearts are seeking. The former can understand the parables of our Lord Jesus, the Sermon on the Mount, and the main stories of the Old Testament. The latter begin to engage with more—such as Augustine's Bible commentaries, or John Calvin's *Institutes*, or the great books of Dr. Timothy Keller.

Is the church in our country ready to face this dangerous secular trend by training and immunizing our young men and women before they go to universities? Are we—clergy, priests, pastors, teachers of the faith—ready to provide such immunization and answer their serious questions?

Do youth in our Christian communities seek the Lord's face so much that he might invite them to devote themselves someday to the service of the gospel? Are the church and Christian ministries playing an effective role among university students? We can do better, and we must.

Reflect

1. What are the arguments for attending a secular university?
2. How can believers preserve their spiritual life in an environment of non-Christian theories?

Between the iPhone and the Nobel

The world has taken great steps forward in recent decades, and we have been witnessing these developments every day of our lives.

Perhaps the greatest tangible evidence of progress is mobile phones, with their relentless versions, announced every few months. In less than two decades since the first appearance of such devices, they have evolved into slim, sophisticated, companionable phones with GPS, games, state-of-the-art cameras, and a variety of helpful utilities and apps.

This remarkable development has led people to place web developers, engineers, and scientists (also recently, medical doctors, due to the COVID-19 world crisis) in increasingly prominent positions, and even form halos over their heads as if they could explore the secrets of the whole universe. They are regarded as our smartest people. People seem to feel that they can understand everything there is to understand in our world.

The problem is, according to many people in scientific and related professions, there is no place for miracles or the supernatural. Scientific theory has become godlike, and it often claims that everything must be proven by experiment, and whatever cannot be proved or determined this way does not exist. Some scholars have argued that since it is impossible to prove the existence of God according to their criteria, this means he does not exist.

Hence, the announcement of the winners of the Nobel Prizes in physics and chemistry a decade ago served to put this arrogance into proper perspective.

In October 2011, the names of the American physicists who discovered that the universe is in a continuous expansion were announced (Saul Perlmutter, Brian P. Schmidt, and Adam G. Riess). Before their research, it had been thought that the movement of planets in nature was constantly slowing down after the Big Bang, and according to Newton's theories of objects' attraction of each other. For many years, physicists had considered the three Newton laws as the basis for movement in nature, but the theory of relativity discovered by Albert Einstein proved that Newton's laws are limited and cannot be applied in all cases. Einstein also concluded that the speed of light is the fastest in the universe. But recently, the velocity of a molecule was recorded higher than the speed of light. The discovery of these Nobel Prize-winning physicists also concluded that there is "black matter" in the universe that makes up seventy percent of the universe and we know nothing about it! Many physicists say that the foundations of Einstein's theory itself have been shaken up and that there is a need now for a new type of physics.

The winner of the chemistry prize was also announced. He is an Israeli Technion scientist, Prof. Daniel Shechtman. He was awarded the prize for the discovery of quasicrystals in solid matter. Before this discovery, scientists used to think that the structure of all crystals is of repeated patterns, but Shechtman found three new types of crystals in matter that do not follow any periodically repeated structure.

God shows over and over again that the universe is so complex and manifold that no one can fully grasp it, despite scientific developments aiming to do so. Scientists are still trying to monitor the movement and structure of the universe despite great progress in every field. But almost as soon as a new theory is introduced, it is refuted. We have recently had a painful reminder of this in the helplessness of the world facing a pandemic. Why is this worth pointing out?

I believe the Lord laughs at our presumptions of power and our arrogance of understanding. He explains to humankind again and again that he is not to be mocked. We should never presume to know very much at all.

God has granted us the grace of contemplating creation, and he desires us to gain more of his greatness by exploring the universe humbly and by attributing glory to him, just as the heavens declare the glory of God and the firmament shows his handiwork.

Reflect

What are some fields of science that despite great advances have been inadequate in understanding the secrets of the universe?

Theology and politics

What we know depends on what we have learned and where we have been.

The thoughts that fill the mind of a Christian are no different. For each of us, the convictions we hold we have gotten often from our families of origin and our upbringing, as well as what we have acquired from our fellowship and learning from friends and teachers, as students, and in our communities. We add to this convictions and concepts that we have studied or read or heard in church from sermons, retreats, and Bible studies—what we call *theology*. The result is the theology and thought that has become the lens through which we see the world.

Thinking that this theology is confined to teaching "spiritual" concepts that do not touch on other aspects of life (such as community, economics, and politics) is wrong.

It is wrong not to admit that our theological views have implications on our political positions. This is true not only for someone like me, who lives in Israel, and not just in the case of end times theology (called "Eschatology"), but for every person and in every country and concerning every field of theology.

The so-called Prosperity Gospel, for example, ignores the different social needs of people and connects in a blunt manner financial blessings and God's pleasure with his people. Whether we like to admit it or not, this theology is more compatible with capitalistic views of the economy that are based on personal and corporate initiative enabling economic success, than with the message of the gospel throughout the New Testament.

Theological views that emphasize one's relationship with God, while neglecting a believer's relationship with his neighbor, have implications too. They often lead to a "non-position," whereby those who hold such views often avoid any involvement in civil society. Then, a state of isolation, which some Christians will wrongly term as "neutrality," prevails. Being "neutral" or "apolitical" is not a non-position but is rather a political support of the status-quo in all its aspects, positive and negative.

This is also true for the local believer in our country, as his or her identity swings between being Arab, Palestinian, Israeli, and Christian—in a country that suffers from national (and maybe religious) conflict. So, those who call for a "neutral" theological position on Israel's theology, for example, have abandoned the ring to other views and isolated themselves from their communities. Such a view enhances and supports the current situation, including the ongoing injustices.

Then there is the theological position concerning God's absolute sovereignty versus the theology that puts more emphasis on the role of human beings. Holders of the first will easily accept institutional changes that are achieved through occupation or a coup; they will see God as sovereign and they will be reluctant to challenge these changes. Supporters of the second will be inclined to see the importance of the active role of believers in opposing or supporting change.

Our view of the kingdom of God, and the role of believers in it, always governs our engagement, or lack thereof, with our communities, cities, and countries in disseminating the values of God's kingdom. If we believe that the kingdom of God requires that we spread its values, then we will call for honesty and clean hands, for example, in all aspects of life. We will demand that these values prevail outside the church and even in government. And those who consider the sovereignty of these values as secondary will likely consider corruption in government as unimportant. According to them, these are the affairs of the world, which have been put under the power of evil, and the believer has a higher calling—that of saving souls.

In the end, every Evangelical claims to apply the whole Bible, although each stresses one aspect of it over others and chooses certain positions over others. My point is this: every emphasis or theological choice has consequences—and we should all be aware of the choices we make.

Reflect

1. How would you describe the relationship between theology and politics?
2. Think of another example of how a change in theology can affect one's political views.

Part Four

The Work of Church

Youth are the future–so how do we reach them?

I n our churches, we often hear that youth are the future, and so we should focus our activities toward them. This is, of course, true. For example, in Palestine, those in the age group 15–29 are 30 percent of the population, and in Israel, people between the ages of 15 and 25 comprise 15 percent of its citizens.

How do we invest in them? How do we address them? In our churches, we spend a good deal of time strategizing this, but I also believe that youth need to appreciate the spirit of the church before any investment in them will make a difference. What is such a spirit?

This generation of youth in my country, and probably in most countries of the world, was born in a more prosperous time than the generations preceding it. It is also a generation that was raised with busy parents, in their careers and in the distractions of modern life, while also valuing the need for their children's academic success. This generation is exposed, in an unprecedented manner, to what is happening in the world, and it interacts with others through social media and the internet at a speed and with an ease that earlier generations could not have fathomed.

Generally, the profile of today's young man or woman is alert, informed, lacking in personal interaction with busy parents, interested in academic success, using modern technology, and closely connected with friends through various devices.

Therefore, if the church wishes to reach out to this generation, and it is compelled to do so if it wants to continue to live, then it must ensure a special environment for youth without compromising its beliefs. Youth will be attracted to the church only if they find there what will fulfill their needs.

Churches should be real in their communications, without hypocrisy or double standards. Youth are idealistic and search for authenticity and despise the fake ways of the world. They look for principles at work. Jesus's principles in the Sermon of the Mount (Matthew 5–7) appeal to them. They demand harmony between doctrine and behavior. According to them, church life has to be comprehensive and holistic.

This generation also looks for a church in which they can find love and real care. They need consideration and a desire from others to know their circumstances—someone to understand their challenges even if they seem odd. They ask for equal terms and criticize what they see as over-superiority. This requires openness to study the needs of young people today without stereotyping and without settling for outdated answers. To respond to life's questions in Bible-based logic, one must have a wide knowledge of the existing culture.

Young people also desire a social, practical implementation for their faith through and with the blessing of the church. Issues of justice, mercy, and social change are paramount. They see these as part of a holistic faith. Since they are so tightly connected to their peers, they seek an external expression of their faith that will have a positive impact for the wider community.

May the Lord help us to bring a unique understanding of church and mission so that we can reach out to this important generation for a blessed future.

Reflect

1. What was your view of the church when you were young? Has it changed since then?
2. Think of examples of things done in churches that make them authentic and real.

A prophet is needed for the people of the prophets

Arabs of this land enjoy the privilege of witnessing the Jewish people as they revive their civil and political life in their country after two thousand years of diaspora. Not only are we watching them closely but we also co-live with them as citizens of one state.

This "coexistence" is taking place at a time when our people are struggling with this state on many fronts. The Jewish people have established their statehood on the ruins of the Palestinian people. Of course, our relationship as Arabs with the Jews of this homeland has many additional layers and complexities beyond what can be written here.

On the other hand, as Evangelical Christians, we believe in the Bible: both the Old and the New Testaments. We study and we know the stories of the fathers like Abraham, Jacob, and Joseph just like we know the stories of Jesus, Paul, and John. Our sermons are taken from the Book of Esther as well as the Book of Philemon. Our devotions tackle the beginnings of creation in Genesis as well as the beginnings of incarnation in the Gospels of Matthew and Luke.

As Evangelicals who love the Old Testament and live among Jews in Israel in the twenty-first century, we have the opportunity to observe the role of the teachings of the Old Testament in the life of the country today. Sometimes we understand the stances of Jews who are socially conservative, but sympathy stops at that point because their extreme attitudes are clearly shown in other walks of life.

Israel has recently been gripped by racism and hatred toward non-Jews, especially Arabs. All of this erupted from religious

Jewish circles that claim to stick to the Torah. They select verses from the Old Testament and take other verses out of context, to explain and support their abhorrent and racist behavior.

Current Jewish leaders here often use passages from the Old Testament and twist them to prevent Arabs from renting houses, or to support building a settlement by looting additional Arab lands. Uptight Jewish young men imagine they are accompanying Joshua the son of Nun in one of his conquests when they attack unarmed Arab boys. For the objective viewer, unfortunately, the more religious the rabbis are, the more they miss true religion and the more ill-mannered and misbehaved they are. It also seems that the less adherent to religion Jews are, the more tolerant and open to peace with Arabs they become. I could safely say that observant Jews in Israel, especially rabbis, are leading most racist campaigns sweeping the country at a time when they claim to keep and apply the teachings of the Torah.

Do we accept this, as Arab Evangelicals? And what is our role at a time when the Bible is used to justify this racism? Are we not also people of the Bible? How is it possible for us to accept their misinterpretation of God's words to justify sin?

There are two different extremes among Arab groups for dealing with these Jewish sins in Israel. The first are those who desire to atone for the crimes committed against Jews over the centuries, especially the Holocaust, and so they always refrain from criticizing Jews in situations today. The second group are those who continually attack the Jews, in large part because they reject the first group's claims.

But there is need for a third group of people who represent the sincere prophetic voice among Arab Christians in Israel—and who see what is happening to us in this land.

We must remind the Jewish people of the commandment in the Torah, "Love your neighbor as yourself" (Leviticus 19:18b). We must show them again the grace that Abraham showed to Lot (Genesis 19). We must talk with them about God's warnings to his people about mistreating the stranger who dwells in their midst (Ezekiel 22:7).

Is there anyone to remind them of the words of the prophet Micah:

> He has shown you, O mortal, what is good. And what does the LORD require of you? To act justly and to love mercy and to walk humbly with your God. (Micah 6:8)

Reflect

1. Think of passages of the Old Testament that instruct us to practice and advocate for social justice.
2. How can we biblically justify a position that criticizes the state of Israel while maintaining a spirit of love?

Do we need constitutions in church?

The Old Testament is distinguished by the Law and the various religious decrees and instructions that placed a heavy burden on those who fell under it. Those who wanted to please the Lord tended to achieve that goal by strictly applying the law to their lives. However, they kept failing one time after another.

The New Testament replaced this Law with the law of love, and thus the Christian age of grace came to rule. Christians are proud that, unlike other religions, they do not turn to harsh and unyielding laws and regulations in their lives, but are given the freedom to live by the Gospel of Christ without such rigidity.

So the Lord established his church without listing precise systems for its practical management. The Lord introduced the principles and functions of ministers, elders, and deacons. However, he did not provide a recipe for the mechanism of decision-making, relationships among church members, or the pastor's relationship with elders. Again, we were given freedom to live by the Gospel, but that sometimes means we may lack clear direction.

The New Testament also introduced general principles of dealing with each other in love and respect, but did not provide specific instructions, mechanisms, or rules of action to arrange and coordinate our corporate lives together as believers. For instance, it does not mention the length of time for the minister's or the deacon's ministry, anything about the budget approval process, how a pastor or deacon or elder should be elected, what the job description of a youth minister ought to include, and how the evaluation of each ministry is done and by whom.

Sometimes, a few more laws—or at least, details—can be helpful!

For these reasons, some churches and church denominations have drafted constitutions and systems to organize their work and achieve its goals and vision. These systems are considered to be as a general framework, but their core is the principles and rules of the Bible. They establish their systems based on prayer, and there should be a majority endorsement so that they become binding. It might sound strange that a church restricts itself by its constitution and is not allowed to set it aside. This is because it is the joint agreement of members on the rules of conduct. A constitution is established after study and prayer. It becomes the supreme authority over the pastor and even above the public meeting unless that same constitution is later amended by a majority of those who approved it in the first place. All of this should be based on the Lord's command that everything be done in a fitting and orderly way (1 Corinthians 14:40).

Therefore, it is necessary to reject claims that are seemingly spiritual, logical, or practical about setting the constitution aside in a particular case—even if it is exceptional. A constitution is supposed to address exceptional cases and what decisions should be made in such cases.

It was once common for Arab groups not to follow fixed systems, but rather, to "play it by ear" without rules, regulations, laws, or organization. This approach is both the cause and the result of backwardness. Chaotic work that depends on moods and tendencies and fleetingly charismatic figures can lead to failure, injustice, dissatisfaction, and weakening of church effectiveness. This same inclination in Arab culture to work lawlessly and "play it by ear" matches the tendency of leaders in some churches not to have constitutions in their churches or to disregard them if they exist. They claim that ministry should be done "freely" and make false claims about God speaking to them, with utter disregard for the systems that the Lord himself has set in place: a constitution through the agreement of the members! At times, they claim that we should not be as Pharisees, adhering to laws, and at other times they say that the Holy Spirit is leading them to things that go beyond the constitution, or that exceptional circumstances oblige the church to get rid of such a yoke!

In most cases, these are untrue justifications so that the leader who calls for exceptions can do whatever they like without a deterrent or an overseer. It violates the agreement between all those who approved and implemented both the regulations and the constitution. It is also a breach of the Lord's command to work in an orderly manner, fulfill our promises, and keep our word.

Reflect

1. Why are by-laws and constitutions important in churches?
2. What might it mean to live the commandments of God without their defining who we are as believers?

Truth for me is being astray from you

I am a Christian," "I am a Muslim," "I am a Maronite," "I am a Shiite," "I am a communist," "I am a capitalist," "I am a patriot. . . ." Lately, we have been hearing these "I am" phrases either literally or indirectly.

Sometimes, they are accompanied by attacks or accusations of infidelity or marginalization, especially on social networks that make it easy to hide behind a screen and degrade *the other*. Such phrases are usually offensive to those who do not belong to the speaker's category. This type of attack, the subsequent counterattack, and the electronic debate where the smoke of the battle reaches to the skies lead to negative consequences. They cause disharmony, hatred, distance, and estrangement among people of every nation.

It is not the mere phrases that are offensive, as they are only an expression of identity and a sense of belonging; but when accompanied by attacking others, the phrases are unacceptable. In reaction, some people have adopted a contradictory attitude. To clarify, they call for irreligiousness or political or social neutrality so that they avoid the rift. Others have adopted a stance of indifference or impartiality. The purpose of these stances or counter-convictions is to meld all individuals into the so-called melting pot of unity. They think that disputes and differences will disappear, and we will all live in unmatched peace.

The best way, however, is neither the former nor the latter.

God has created each one of us uniquely. We are of different nationalities, identities, languages, and characters. This diversity adds beauty to the lives of people. The people of China look monotonous and similar to some of us, and probably we all look strangely alike to them. I can only speak for Israel, where the diversity is striking: there is the secular and the religious Jew (in their different denominations); Arabs of various sects in villages, cities, and mixed cities; Bedouins, and many others. The style of buildings and work differ throughout the country: villages of Galilee over the high mountains, the Kibbutzim, the Jewish cities on the coast, Jerusalem, Eilat, and the Negev towns—they all show remarkable diversity.

The emphasis that any of us places on our personal identity does not necessarily mean rejecting others and despising them. *The other* is God's creation, just like you, and their stances often stem from their position, circumstances, and identity. Despite the strong convictions spread in our country, it should be rather controlled by the conviction of pluralism and personal freedom, even if my religious conviction is uncompromising. For instance, I am not ashamed to be a Christian who strongly believes in a well-established, adamant creed on which I base my worldview. Nonetheless, this does not mean imposing my opinion or using coercion by physical or verbal violence so that *the other* accepts and adopts what I believe in. The main principle here is to adhere firmly to your conviction, yet to be flexible in your behavior and in dealing with others.

Those of holistic religious or ideological convictions attribute their harsh treatment of *the other* to their faith and belief, which is often the real problem. For them, the creed they believe in claims the absolute right that the entire world must accept, believe in, and abide by. The followers of such faiths will do their best to bring the light that they claim to have found to those who have missed it or to impose the teachings of that light on every spot and every person who is astray on this earth. However, they forget that our fellow humans have the right to adopt the status or the creed of being "astray." It is my right to try to persuade them of the futility of their being astray, but this should be done in friendliness and without coercion. Forcing anyone to accept my conviction means depriving them of their humanity, which is manifested in their freedom.

A person without freedom is just a speaking animal. By forcing them, you oppose the purpose of God himself, whom you claim to worship, because God does not want us to worship him reluctantly. He has created human beings, not machines or robots programmed to follow him. At the end of the day, and regardless of our views, truth for me is being astray for my brother, and being astray for him is truth for me! We will never know which one of us is right. A third opinion is that we are both wrong, or both right, until death. Some points of view would even claim that we will not know the truth for sure even after death. I think differently.

If your faith rejects the idea that personal freedom is a fundamental principle of life, then you should examine and re-evaluate it. The god who calls for coercion or murder to spread the "light" and defeat "darkness" is a truly awful god who deserves no honor. The ideology that desires oppression and imposition deserves to be rejected. These religions or ideologies will lead only to an eternal war in which the individuals of our peoples, our parties, and our religions will kill each other alternately—may God forbid!

Reflect

Are there areas in which a believer can't accept someone else's view in the name of freedom of speech? What are they?

Autopilot and Christian thought

Imagine driving your car with your mind fully occupied to the extent that you do not concentrate on the details of the road. Eventually and surprisingly, you find that you have already arrived at your home. Has this ever happened to you?

I usually wake up in the morning, answer the call of nature, wash my face, shave, and get dressed, while at the same time heating the water to make my coffee. I do all this in successive mechanical processes, like a habit, that I never think much about.

These human mechanical processes are sometimes called "autopilot" because they are similar to the work of a device of the same name in an aircraft that guides and directs the plane without the need for human help. They do not require effort, and we perform them without thinking because we follow a certain manner to which we are accustomed. The routine nature of it, the very unthinkingness of it, makes it easier for us to accomplish multiple things at once.

This phenomenon of operating on autopilot has spread inside the church and in the spiritual life, as well. It comes in the form of thinking, or non-thinking, patterns. There are clichés we now use that appear when we are worshiping or in prayer. We use them without thinking.

Some of the simplest matters in the church follow this pattern as well. For example, some say that the church service must begin with reading a psalm, and we cannot deviate from this pattern. Any change would destabilize the service, as if it is one of the fundamentals of faith and belief. It's hard for me to watch the church operating on autopilot. What could be wrong if a church service started with a reading from Philippians instead of a psalm? Is there a biblical basis for that objection, or is it just intellectual laziness or rigid attitudes?

Sometimes, this concept goes beyond mere habits to more conceptual matters. For instance, some in our church seem to believe that we could never learn from other churches (Evangelical or otherwise). This is intellectual laziness, arrogance, or boastfulness. Some hold onto the same visual aids and the same kind of preaching despite changes of time and changes of place. How can an audience who keeps a smartphone in their pockets accept the same style of preaching as one who knew nothing of such technology? Is the lazy autopilot preventing progress, change, and creativity?

Sometimes this fossilized pattern infiltrates even our theology and beliefs. Of course, there are foundations and constants of faith that are nonnegotiable such as the divinity of Christ, the Crucifixion, the Resurrection, salvation, and the infallibility of the Bible. However, some doctrines have been taught to us for years, and thus, it is difficult to restudy or rediscuss them due to the same intellectual rigidity. This includes subjects such as the teaching about the last days, the effectiveness of spiritual talents, the role of the Holy Spirit, or topics that the church avoids such as its role in society in answering questions regarding justice, peacemaking, and poverty.

We need to replace the autopilot in our lives with creative human pilots who will fly high in the space of life and glorify God through research, development, and change.

Reflect

Think of examples of autopilot behaviors in your personal life and church life. How can we deactivate this autopilot?

RIP, may you have long days!

The phone rings. The voice on the other end is low and choked with grief, as though speaking from the bottom of a deep well.

Friend: "How are you? Have you heard the news?"
Me: "No, what news?"
Friend: "Abu Samaan El Khalidy has passed away."
Me: "Poor man! He suffered so much. When is the funeral?"
Friend: "Tomorrow at three o'clock at the town church."
Me: "May you have long days!"

Abu Samaan lived seventy-six years; he was a member of the denomination but rarely attended church meetings or participated in its activities or prayers. He lived an ordinary life, and in the eyes of the people, he was a good man and well respected. This is except for two things that disrupted his life. The first was his fondness for alcohol, especially Arak, which affected his relationship with his wife and family. Several times, his neighbors heard him shout at his family while drunk, swaying in his walk. During the last years of his life, he started to drink less because of liver illness. The second thing that disrupted his life was his quarrel with his younger brother on the size and portion of a piece of land they inherited from their father. Unfortunately, Abu Samaan did not get the chance to reconcile with his brother before his death. What an embarrassing and painful situation after death! Now, the estrangement will continue between the offspring of the two brothers. Blood is not thicker than water in this family, because of hardened hearts and the love of money.

People come from north and south, from east and west, to practice the verse, "Rejoice with those who rejoice, and weep with those who weep." All roads of the town lead to the church, and there is the funeral.

A stranger would be astonished to see all those men and women who were able to leave their work, jobs, and errands to gather at the church in the middle of a weekday, with only short notice. Many wear sunglasses and stand in the courtyard outside. Men are happy about the social gathering, so they chat with each other. Now and then, you hear a light laugh. Women silently sit in the hall around the body. Abu Samaan's wife, her daughters, and her daughters-in-law weep silently. They had expected his death weeks earlier, but no one ever knows the specific hour, so it is always a surprise. Death is like a thief in the night. The rest of the women sit quietly or speak softly, watching the comers and goers. They are all dressed in black; they are pale and without makeup, but that's one of the few things they have in common. The various outfits and the different behaviors are clear despite the overwhelmingly black color of their clothing. They are grateful for the opportunity to catch up with each other, to hear what's been happening in everyone's lives.

Now, it is time. The priest leads some men into the hall where the coffin sits. When the men enter the room, immediately the weeping and wailing voices increase, and the farewell cries of the deceased's daughters are raised as if one had turned up the volume of a TV.

The priest recites a short prayer, and nods, giving the signal that the time has come for the moment of the last farewell. Those closest to the coffin stand in something like a queue to bid farewell, and some kiss the deceased. It is a cold kiss that does not express real passion or true grief and suffering.

Time is short; the room is very hot and overcrowded. The body had been kept in the morgue for about a day. Patience is limited, and within an hour, the priest needs to go for a wedding in a neighboring village. They separate Um Samaan gently from her life companion; the couple has lived together for forty-nine years. Truly, only death was able to part them. Soon, the coffin is closed, and young men rush forward to carry it into the church.

The body is now in the middle of the church. I have always amusingly wondered: does not the deceased feel tired, lying on his back? Maybe he wishes to rise quickly, like someone who has been suddenly burned by fire, to examine those who are crying from their hearts, and those who only pretend to do so.

Abu Samaan is an ordinary person from a humble family, so the Mass is led only by the parish priest. If the deceased were of higher financial and political importance, you'd find several priests sharing in the Mass. And if the deceased were even luckier, you might find a bishop sharing in the service, as well. Our priest recites the prayers mechanically. Clearly, he's done this many times before. Within twenty-three minutes and a few seconds, Abouna ("Father") has absolved him from his sins and placed him in the ranks of the saints.

Once again, young men proceed to carry the coffin, heading to the cemetery. The big challenge now is how to all walk at the same speed. . . . Some of them move rapidly, while others languish, burdened by grief and the weight of the coffin.

They arrive at the El-Khaledy family section of the cemetery. The verse "from dust to dust" no longer applies to modern cemeteries, as coffins are put in building structures like cupboards with drawers. The priest prays an extra prayer to make sure the deceased is safe in the heavenly realms. As for the body, as the weather starts to get warmer, it will be laid in another place: in the next-to-last drawer at the top of the building.

The children of the deceased, his brothers, his sisters, and his relatives stand in the long queue to receive condolences. The phrase "may he rest in peace" comes out of every mouth. The active among the mourners hurry up to offer their condolences first so they can fly back to their cars to return to work and homes before the traffic congestion builds.

I wonder: *Have we accomplished our duty toward Abu Samaan and showed respect to his children? Have we heard a word of condolence at the funeral? Did we hear an encouragement to the mourners to live a life of righteousness and faith? Have we heard anything about hope after death?* None.

Amid my many questions, I remember that we have to go this week to offer condolences one more time at the family house. I don't remember what time they asked people to arrive.

Reflect

1. Does your community have its own unique funeral traditions?
2. What do you think the author was trying to convey?

The new Evangelical rituals

Believers of Free Evangelical Churches here in Israel are reserved in using the term "religion" or to define themselves as "religious." This is because religion is defined as a system of doctrines that prescribe patterns of behavior and commands that are characterized by rituals of inherited, repeated tradition.

Because of our faith in personal renewal and new birth, our freedom in Christ, and the inspiration of the Word of God, Evangelicals tend to reject religious ritual. Therefore, we refrain from using the term "religion" and instead use "faith"; instead of "religious" we use "believer," "disciple," or "Christian."

However, our Evangelical Christian life doesn't lack signs of religiosity. Patterns of religiosity have sneaked into our churches. This is negative in terms of the formal external aspects of how churches function, and unfortunately, also in the matter of the essential internal practices of our faith.

In the formal aspect of worship, we have created patterns for worship and prayer services. These patterns of speech and terminology are often repeated in language so that they become meaningless in the minds of those who speak them and listen to them. Hymns and songs are indeed varied, and there is freedom in their selection and singing, but they are often chanted mechanically without their words being pondered, and without meditation on the deep and blessed meanings of them.

Furthermore, in terms of the essential internal practices of faith, religiosity has sneaked into our worship. We sing, pray, and listen to the Word, but do we forget that getting close to God is not a magical process that takes place after rites of routine and occasionally emotional gestures? Those who attend worship often think that the more we practice those rituals, the closer we come to God or even unite with God. But true worship and drawing nearer to God can't be achieved without fulfillment of the conditions set by the Bible. Unfortunately, we have often neglected these conditions, such as these:

Personal faithfulness and holiness

"Who may ascend the mountain of the LORD? Who may stand in his holy place? The one who has clean hands and a pure heart, who does not trust in an idol or swear by a false god." (Psalm 24:3–4)

Reconciliation

"Therefore, if you are offering your gift at the altar and there remember that your brother or sister has something against you, leave your gift there in front of the altar. First, go and be reconciled to them; then come and offer your gift." (Matthew 5:23–24)

Forgiveness

"And when you stand praying, if you hold anything against anyone, forgive them, so that your Father in heaven may forgive you your sins." (Mark 11:25)

Standing for justice and victory for the oppressed

"When you spread out your hands in prayer, I hide my eyes from you; even when you offer many prayers, I am not listening. Your hands are full of blood! Wash and make yourselves clean. Take your evil deeds out of my sight; stop doing wrong. Learn to do right; seek justice. Defend the oppressed. Take up the cause of the fatherless; plead the case of the widow." (Isaiah 1:15–18)

In our churches, we rarely talk about the things that are required of the believer in his daily life: being honest in work, being compassionate in relationships with others, dealing with authorities, being wise in managing money, and so on. We keep our conversation "spiritual"—but it is powerless.

Unfortunately, in many cases we have neglected the above-mentioned requests of the Lord as a condition of true worship and jumped directly to the rituals—that are supposed to bring us to a state of spiritual ecstasy. Without these conditions, they are just emotions, movements, and rituals that are empty and unacceptable, as the Lord says in the verses above. Some of us have suffered from the illness of religiosity in its new Evangelical manifestation and have neglected what the Word of God says about worship in spirit and truth.

Reflect

1. What Evangelical rituals have you recently observed?
2. Are rituals in worship ever helpful?

Lest we lose compassion

Recent events in Gaza, after the move of the American Embassy to Jerusalem in May 2018, resulted in the killing of sixty people and the inflicting of injuries to thousands within two days. These horrific events gave rise to many questions. Yet, what drew my attention was not the political, doctrinal, or historical aspects of the situation, but this question: What kind of emotion do these events stir in us as Christians, and are these emotions justified?

I'll approach the question from the perspective of the cornerstone himself—our Lord Jesus—as he is the example we should follow.

Jesus is love. He gave his life and humbled himself to die as a slave while being the King of Kings. He is pure love; there is nothing like this love anywhere else, or in anyone else, in the world. In addition to this indescribable love—shown on the cross for all sinners—he also expressed his love, mercy, and compassion to humankind while on this earth. He did not hide his emotions: he cried at the tomb of his friend Lazarus, and he wept over Jerusalem when he foretold its future from the Mount of Olives. Unlike the legalists who were emotionless, Jesus looked at people with compassion and sympathy. He looked at the rich young man and loved him (Mark 10:21). When he saw the crowds, he had compassion on them (Matthew 9:36). He went about healing people and casting out demons, all stemming from a heart full of love. Seeing the needs of people, their misery, pain, and distress, he worked to remove these. This was the mission that he claimed at the beginning of his ministry in the synagogue in Nazareth: to help the poor, to heal the brokenhearted, to preach release to the captive, to give sight to the blind, and to liberate the oppressed (Luke 4:18).

One of the characteristics that the apostle Paul predicts for the end of time is that people will become without affection (2 Timothy 3:3). The question is, did this enter just recently into the people of Christ, who have long been characterized by tenderness and compassion and distinguished by initiatives and projects that have provided help and mercy to all people regardless of race or religion? Christians have been known through the ages for loving their neighbor, following the example of their Master, traveling to all corners of the earth to spread knowledge where ignorance prevails, and providing healthcare where illness and disease are widespread. For these causes, they have built schools, universities, hospitals, elderly homes, shelters for battered women, orphans, the handicapped, the homeless, and many more misfortunate people.

It is regrettable to see the absence of this kind of compassion in the ongoing tragedy of Gaza. There, we see many hungry people, rampant unemployment, poverty, unsafe drinking water, intermittent access to basic electricity, and travel bans that keep people from easily moving around where they live and work. And despite all these things, we are witnessing the obliteration of the mercy of Christians because of prejudices, political justifications, and religious differences. Sometimes these conditions suffocate mercy, either by repressing it, hiding it, or making it selective: it is for certain people or nations only. Yet, this contradicts the commandment of the Lord, who commanded us to love, and to love everyone equally (Luke 6:32–36).

Some justify this lack of compassion and sympathy for the people of Gaza by blaming them for demonstrating against Israel or for wanting to cross the barrier by force. Some would claim that they were incited by Hamas or that they supported or participated in aggressive operations in the past. However, the worst is the way some would draw their justification from the world of the unseen or scenarios of the end times.

Do any of these reasons justify the killing of human beings? Do any of those justify taking away a life that the Almighty has given? Does any of these justifications make it legitimate to take away souls created in the image of God and his likeness?

Moreover, aren't we all sinners? Does one error justify another?

May the Lord remove the layers of justification that have blurred human sight and caused human compassion to slumber, so that we may be merciful and loving as our Savior, and be kind to others without selectivity and with great love let the world know that we are his disciples.

Reflect

What can we do to keep compassion and tenderness alive in our hearts despite the difficult events that we are exposed to?

Loving the neighbor in the Holy Land

Millions of believers of every religion say that they love their God. They declare their love by strictly following their laws. If you love someone, you will do whatever it takes to satisfy them and make them happy. In Christianity, the Lord Jesus gave another commandment that he considered to be like the commandment of the love of God:

> One of them, an expert in the law, tested him with this question: "Teacher, which is the greatest commandment in the Law?" Jesus replied: "'Love the Lord your God with all your heart and with all your soul and with all your mind.' This is the first and greatest commandment. And the second is like it: 'Love your neighbor as yourself.' All the Law and the Prophets hang on these two commandments." (Matthew 22:35–40)

One wonders how it is possible to love people as we love God: to put the love of our limited, mortal, sinful brothers and sisters in the same category as loving our eternal, limitless Creator and Savior who blessed us with all goodness. Why has the Lord given the utmost importance to the love of neighbor by placing it on a similar level to the love of God? This is because the love of the neighbor is a clear and apparent proof of our love to God:

> Whoever claims to love God yet hates a brother or sister is a liar. For whoever does not love their brother and sister, whom they have seen, cannot love God, whom they have not seen. And he has given us this command: Anyone who loves God must also love their brother and sister. (1 John 4:20–21)

Since God has created us in his image and likeness (Genesis 1:26–27), we cannot love God if we do not love his image and likeness. External appearance is not what is referred to here; rather, we are called to love a person because they are a human created in the image of God.

After the Lord declared these two greatest commandments, he was asked, "Who is my neighbor?" (Luke 10:25–37). Jesus answered indirectly by using the parable of the Good Samaritan, and according to the parable, the neighbor included even a person's worst enemy.

Jesus was speaking to a Jew and using as an example the Samaritan people, who were enemies of the Jews at the time. They were two opposing and conflicting peoples both in their faith and style of life. How could the meaning of this parable be applied on a personal and public level now, especially in Christ's Church in the Holy Land, where we are called to love our neighbor as ourselves? How can we do that?

The Lord explained the meaning of the love he requests when he likened Christ's relationship with the church to a man's relationship with his wife. He said, "After all, no one ever hated their own body, but they feed and care for their body, just as Christ does the church" (Ephesians 5:29). It is that kind of love that seeks its own interest while seeking the interest of others. The love of ourselves does not take priority over the wellbeing of others. We give others due respect and esteem just as we seek our own good and our own edification. We should not consider ourselves better than they are, but regard all as valuable people in the eyes of God, who created them in his image and likeness.

The love of others required of us as Holy Land Christians means that we are concerned for the welfare of all people. It means responsibility toward others and not just leaving them alone. This requires helping others not to harm themselves or others. It means that we refuse to have bias for certain people based on sect, ethnicity, nationality, religion, or language. It means not only standing with the oppressed and the persecuted but also stopping the oppressor because, by his oppression, he marginalizes the image of God inside himself.

We have to work diligently to translate our love for the Lord as Christians into this kind of love for all our neighbors.

Reflect

1. What perspective can help us love others as God requires of us?

2. Do we risk alienating others when we do not try to know people's real interests?

Hidden fundamentalism is ravaging our message

The Free Evangelical churches or Bible churches regard the entire Bible as the Word of God. They preach Scripture and request the commitment of their followers to its teachings. They consider themselves as ones who follow the approach of the early church in simplicity of ministry and commitment to the Word of God.

However, the Evangelical churches are not the only churches who make these claims. All churches consider themselves one way or another as successors to, or in a direct line from, the first church as told in the book of Acts, and the legitimate heirs of Christ's Great Commission.

What is it that defines an Evangelical church from one that is not Evangelical? Claiming a connection to the earliest expressions of Christianity is not going to be enough.

The answer revolves around the use of the word *fundamentalist*.

A Christian liberal trend appeared about a century ago that threatened the authenticity of Scripture. This trend claimed that the Bible was not inspired by God. Liberal Christians began to point to portions of the text, focusing most of all on the miracle stories, saying that a modern person can no longer accept the supernatural side of these accounts. They began to subtly palliate some of the biblical revelations to the extent that they almost canceled the concept of Christ's salvation—gone was the Virgin birth, and gone was the truth of the Resurrection.

This led to a reaction of Evangelicals, as they returned to the fundamentals and origins of faith. They began to state these clearly—again, for all to see and hear. And "fundamentalism" soon acquired a negative meaning, even though it was intended as an impenetrable shield and as a protection of the true faith from attacks by other groups.

Today, only a minority of Evangelicals describe themselves also as "fundamentalists"; we usually replace that name with others such as "conservatives" or "Bible-believers." Decades have passed since that initial rise of Evangelical fundamentalism, but its imprint remains tangible. It is this influence and resorting to the fundamentals of the faith that determines today the focus of Free Evangelical churches in the Middle East, and similar Evangelical branches of the faith found elsewhere around the world.

The Bible offers not only doctrine and faith but also principles of life for those who believe. The churches that adopted liberal theology have emphasized social work while being overly permissive in matters of doctrine. In some Evangelical churches, the focus on the "social gospel" (social involvement and activism with the poor in fighting injustice) has become a mockery because it is a reminder that these churches are distancing themselves from the proper teaching of the Word of God. Meanwhile, fundamentalists feel that they are the protectors of the faith and that without them, true faith would be lost in apostasy.

But fundamentalists are not blameless, either. They have too often lost the blessing of experiencing the depth and perfection of the Christian life.

For example, they become displeased with the idea of adding works as an equal element to faith as necessary for salvation. Hence, they refrain from preaching and teaching about the life of holiness (honesty, integrity, and faithfulness) to block the path for those who believe that the commitment to the life of holiness is one of gaining salvation. Thus, they create a gap in the life of faith.

They have also resented liberals' criticism of the Word of God. This causes them to adhere to a too-literal interpretation of the Word, as a reaction. They then misinterpret passages that do not stand up to literal interpretation. Furthermore, because they see the negative ramifications of the "social gospel," they abandon helping the needy in their communities in favor of focusing only on evangelism and discipleship. They forget that Jesus himself performed healing actions and fed the poor (Acts 10:38). They resent liberals turning Jesus into a political activist, so they reject the social mission of Jesus, who was also concerned with justice (Luke 4:18, Isaiah 61, Micah 6: 8, among others). In this way, the approach of many churches has become reactionary to those who misrepresent the full gospel, but ironically enough, these same churches have diminished the full truth of Scripture themselves.

There is a better way.

It is time to review the current Evangelical approach and put fundamentalism in its proper, limited place. Unrestrained fundamentalism that stems from the fear of losing faith will inevitably lead to devastation and will prevent Christians from accomplishing their proper role in the kingdom of God now and in the future.

Reflect

1. What are some positive things about fundamentalism?
2. How can we move past a reactionary fundamentalist approach to an intentional, holistic view of Scripture?

Unhidden camera

The kid gets his face dirty with cake rich in cream. His parents are amused, so they take a photo of him and post it on their Facebook accounts a few seconds later.

In one of our Arab villages during an extremely hot summer, a verbal quarrel takes place, soon turning into a fight with hands, sticks, and knives, and victims fall. Police and first aid paramedics rush in while more villagers are ready to engage in the fight. Local websites quickly publish photos and videos of victims of the fight in all its gory details. They are now available for everybody to see, far or near, while spilled blood hasn't yet dried from the street.

The media's reach is now instant and enormous. It has become so easy and affordable.

Consequently, this quote seems to be the mantra of our lives: "Doing something without posting about it is as if you have not done it at all." Christians are no different, and churches believe it is important to publish their activities, events, and photos on the internet to attract attendees and "followers."

However, the easy publishing and posting of photos and news has raised questions regarding privacy. Every teenager with a mobile phone can publish whatever they want, whenever they want. Should we be so quick to show ourselves at church—in prayer? The Lord urges us in the greatest sermon in history:

> But when you pray, go into your room, close the door and pray to your Father, who is unseen. Then your Father, who sees what is done in secret, will reward you. (Matthew 6:6)

The encouragement here is not limited to prayer in secret, but it extends to giving charity and to fasting as well.

Jesus emphasized the importance of genuine spiritual depth, and he abhorred outward appearances and hypocrisy.

Using cameras often infringes on privacy and makes true spiritual worship difficult. A person may attend a church in order to worship, but then cameras focus on him and others, attacking them from every side, searching for the best effective shot. A genuine worshiper is bound to be distracted by phone clicks and camera shutters. Even further, if one's worship is captured in a "perfect angle," then they might find that photograph published on every concerned site. (And worshipers may begin to concern themselves more with the "perfect angle" of prayer, rather than prayer itself.)

Consider another sensitive example: Is it appropriate to publish photos of the service of washing feet? This is an act that aims to replicate the humbleness of the Lord and includes a certain level of spiritual intimacy. Is it proper to publish it?

Is it possible to concentrate on worshiping the Lord while cameras are stalking attendees? Another tragic irony is that some photographers think they are invisible, so they often get too close to people. Is it possible to preserve the holiness of prayer or preaching while photographers race to take photos? We need ethical standards of privacy to govern this aspect of our worshiping lives—which are changing every day!

Reflect

How do you feel about people using phones during worship
　services?

Six results of church isolation

Many factors can lead to churches living in silos and isolating themselves from the society in which they are planted. Some of these factors are social while others are due to the misinterpretation of a few Bible passages.

The consequences of this isolation are dire and could be summarized as follows:

1. Contradicting the will of the Lord, who showed himself a model of interaction and engagement with people, eating and drinking with ordinary people as well as the elite, and conversing with them. Jesus Christ explicitly asked Christians to be light to the world.

2. Loss of effectiveness: isolation of the church deprives opportunities for the Lord to bless Christians and non-Christians both. The church is supposed to be the arm of the Lord and his voice. If it is far away, how does the church affect people's lives?

3. Creating in people's minds a distorted view of both church and God. If Christians move away from people's concerns and dreams, people form the idea that the church is a mystical or spiritual movement, at best, perhaps irrelevant to their lives. People then regard the church as self-centered—contrary to what Jesus said it should be. People see that the church is not interested in people, lives only between the walls of its buildings, and has lost compassion. This all leads, then, to a distortion of the image of God in their eyes. If people see that the church is disgusted with

them and asks them to keep their problems away from her, then they will reject her and reject her God.

4. Living in a vacuum: Christians tend to spend their time dealing only with their own problems, rivalries, and conflicts. The years are wasted in human machinations instead of in missional activities, interacting with the community and working to bring people closer to the living God. The values of the kingdom of God go uncommunicated and unseen.

5. Society does not enjoy the light and truth that God has bestowed on the church, and thus society plunges deeper into the darkness of ignorance or vain human philosophies.

6. People begin to think that Christ's church has no answers to the modern world and that it is an institution without relevance to modern concerns. An institution lacking answers is perceived as irrelevant and thus loses its voice.

The demand of the hour is the rising of the twenty-first-century church from the tomb to declare that isolation is not an option and that our message, touch, and prophetic voice need to reach the world.

Reflect

1. Why do you think some leaders act to isolate their churches?
2. Can you think of any other negative results of Christian self-isolation?

Beware of money

Throughout history, Christians have regarded their greatest enemy to be atheistic theories and philosophies, or other religions that disagree with Christianity in theology, practice, or values.

It was easy for the stronghold of Christian thought in Europe and America to promote this idea. However, such a view neglected another malicious enemy of the faith: the spirit of materialism and capitalism. Often, European and American Christians did not only ignore such spirit, but they also reconciled with it, laundered it, and even let it into the church.

We were influenced by this thought in the Holy Land and considered it an ally of Christian culture. What is wrong with working hard, earning money, spending it, purchasing homes and cars, traveling leisurely abroad, and living a "comfortable" life?

We justified such a life. We wondered: what is wrong with a man working hard and earning profits from his work? Why can't one get his bread (his cake, his fondue, and his croissant) by the sweat of his brow?

Capitalism and the free economy brought with them moral devastation that sneaked into our lives without being noticed. A citizen in a country that applies capitalism (Israel is certainly at the forefront of its supporters) is working day and night to earn the most they can. They earn more so that people hold them in higher esteem: this is a direct relationship. As their credit balance increases at the bank, so does their level of respect and appreciation from others. And as they work hard to gain more, demands also increase upon them: it is a vicious circle.

The appetite for more does not know any satisfaction, since so many luxuries have become essentials. "Give us this day our daily bread" has become "and also . . . frequent vacations, the latest smartphone, and some really fine automobiles." Money has become a goal and not a means to earn a living. One irony is that because of the long hours of work usually needed to earn more money, there is no time to enjoy what that money can purchase, and then there is no room for God anymore either.

Cheating has even become common in our world where the ends justify the means. After all, we're absolutely convinced that we must have all that stuff.

Society's role models are the rich; people rarely ask how they got their money, and no one cares about their character as long as they are rich. In churches, we sometimes now see similar patterns. The new god is entertainment and leisure, and whoever makes use of them in a way that dazzles the eyes earns the admiration of everyone.

In some Western countries, this same extremist spirit of individualistic capitalism has also led to the crushing of the poor, the sick, and the disabled, and has caused the gap to widen between the rich and the poor.

But whoever meditates on the life of Jesus and the ways of the early church can easily understand what is wrong with all of this. Our Creator, who knows the human heart, hits the nail on the head when he says:

No one can serve two masters. Either you will hate the one and love the other, or you will be devoted to the one and despise the other. You cannot serve both God and money. (Luke 16:13)

To all who consider themselves servants of Jesus Christ—which is the greatest of all honors—beware of money!

Reflect

Isn't this materialistic spirit actually the spirit of freedom and personal accountability? If the answer is yes, then why does it go wrong?

Ten questions on being subject to governing authorities

The words of Scripture must be interpreted in light of their context and the essence of the related subject, taking into consideration other passages that tackle the same topic.

This applies to the interpretation of verses concerning being subject to governing authorities. For example:

> Let everyone be subject to the governing authorities, for there is no authority except that which God has established. The authorities that exist have been established by God. Consequently, whoever rebels against the authority is rebelling against what God has instituted, and those who do so will bring judgment on themselves. For rulers hold no terror for those who do right, but for those who do wrong. Do you want to be free from fear of the one in authority? Then do what is right and you will be commended. (Romans 13:1–3)

The misinterpretation of these verses can allow misusing them to protect unjust governments and policies from legitimate criticism. Furthermore, misinterpretation may motivate people to follow an approach of compliance and acceptance of any government policy or decision without question, or to support immorality and decisions that are in direct contrast to God and his kingdom. This leads to earthly citizenship that is not in keeping with that required by our heavenly citizenship.

The following are ten short objections and questions that can be raised to discern what to do in this area of our lives:

1) Does Romans 13 require only the citizens of the state under a particular government to submit to it, or does it also include those who are not citizens of that state, yet occupants of that governed land?

2) What does Romans 13 mean when it mentions "governing authorities"? Does it refer to instructions and guidelines of the United Nations, the European Union, or NATO? Are we to be subject to supreme world authorities or to the governmental decisions of a given state? To clarify, should UN resolutions adopted and supported by a large number of countries, be applied? Do we have to submit to these authorities, which are comprehensive and international in scope, or only to the governments of individual countries, knowing that the decisions of the first may contradict those of the second?

3) What about popular resistance movements in a country? If the majority of people agree with a movement's goals, who is then considered the supreme authority to be subjected to? Or should the government that rules with the power of arms, even if contrary to the will of the majority, always be the power to which we are subject?

4) If a state includes three powers: executive, legislative, and judicial, and they disagree—which one is meant when we are asked to submit to the governing authorities? The judiciary can veto government decisions and even nullify laws enacted by the legislature if they contradict the constitution. Which authority is right when they are contradicting each other?

5) The contemporary meaning of "governing authorities" in principle, in an era such as ours, is a democratically elected

state. Isn't the constitution, then, the highest authority in the land?

6) The executive governing authority in a democratic state is the principal actor in the rule of law. According to principle, such an authority is allowed to do only what the law entitles him or her to do. Must I then be subject to a ruler who may act without authorization from the law?

7) Does being subject to governing authorities perhaps mean to respect the government institution, but not necessarily the individuals who govern it? If so, the objection to a certain unjust government is not a violation of the general principle of Romans 13. In my opinion, submission is to the institution itself but not to its tyranny. Rebelling against tyrants can be obedience to God depending on how it is done.

8) I believe that what is written in Romans should be understood in light of 1 Peter 2:13a: "Submit yourselves for the Lord's sake to every human authority." Consider how this relates to Romans 13:4, where the ruler is referred to this way: "For he is God's servant for your good." Based on this comparison, some are convinced that the phrase "for the Lord" is a condition of submission. If the authority is evil and does not rule fairly and properly, because it legislates biased systems, then it is not just or correct to follow it. In other words, you do not have to submit to evil laws "for the Lord's sake" or to laws that are not "good."

9) When the soldiers asked the apostles not to preach the gospel, Peter and the apostles answered: "We must obey God rather than human beings!" (Acts 5:29). In other words, Peter and the apostles laid down an

important principle concerning obedience to the various commandments. When the commandments of God contradict the commandments of rulers, we must submit to the first. So, we should disobey a ruler when he decides to discriminate or take actions that oppose justice, because God has ordered us otherwise.

10) Gideon, Barak, and Samson were involved in overthrowing the rulers of the oppressors, yet their names are mentioned as heroes of faith in Hebrews 11. How would they be regarded as heroes of faith if their actions were contrary to God's commandment to be subject to the governing authorities? The settlement of this apparent contradiction requires us to carefully and thoughtfully interpret the commandment of being "subject to the governing authorities" in Romans 13.

Reflect

1. Why do you think the Bible says it is necessary to be subject to the governing authorities?

2. How do you discern when to do as the Bible asks us to do, and when it is legitimate to criticize and depart from the government or its policies?

God saw what he had made wasn't "very good" anymore

The respected daily newspaper *Ha'aretz*, published in Hebrew, said on November 16, 2017, that the previous forty years had seen a dramatic decline of more than fifty percent in Western men's fertility, and that this may threaten the human race with extinction. The article included information showing that this deterioration is not confined to the citizens of developed countries but remains a global phenomenon. The article, quoting research by world-class scientists studying the phenomenon, also pointed out a similar trend among women.

Anyone familiar with the findings of research in the field would conclude that this phenomenon is complex on different levels: physiological, psychological, and environmental. The article mentioned many reasons behind low fertility, starting with the toxic substances that are sprayed to prevent insects from infecting vegetables and fruits, smoking, cell phone radiation, and increased heat, with global warming causing higher temperatures.

Interestingly, the researchers specified that environmental causes were one of the top causes of low fertility because disruption in the environment generates anxiety, fear, and confusion, causing people to "protect" themselves by not giving birth to a new soul that would exist in a polluted, destroyed environment that they themselves are uncomfortable in. Humans subconsciously can create low infertility in their bodies.

Facing this grim scene, one can notice a common cause of this human misery: it is all related to technological "developments" that are causing environmental destruction.

God entrusted the natural environment to our care, but human selfishness has been destroying it. Greedy businesspeople don't want to incur the expense of disposing of waste properly and safely. The tools to do so are often unavailable and government authority is not forcing them to make environment-friendly decisions. Sometimes, when there are restricting laws and regulations for companies, they remain only ink on paper and are not implemented because of morally questionable agreements between owners of companies and politicians. When people are distracted by their momentary benefit, no one will realize the long-term necessity of taking care of God's creation.

Also problematic is the insane and irresponsible rush toward technological progress that produces stress and careless disregard of dire consequences. Cell phones and human beings have become inseparable, and because of this we generally disregard the damage created by mining for their materials, producing these products, and then the aforementioned heat and radiation they put out. Air conditioners also are a problem; they contribute to the depletion of the ozone layer and are nevertheless more and more widely and indiscriminately used. Unfortunately, no less harmful alternatives to the environment are being tested. All this leads to global warming and changes in the atmosphere that the Lord has made with matchless precision. It also causes turbulence to different organisms, resulting in fertility decline.

It often seems that Christians do not take God's command to preserve the environment and the world that God has created seriously. When God created our world, he saw that everything was very good. Then he created human beings and entrusted them with that amazing planet. But we have become distracted.

We should remember that one way we can spread God's kingdom is by taking care of his creation. The church is supposed to raise its voice to awaken people and remind them of the importance of doing God's work on earth—in this case, maintaining the health of our environment. This will bring glory to God.

Reflect

Has the spread of the COVID-19 pandemic and its consequences taught us anything about the environment and our responsibilities as Christians?

Listen to the beat of the street

I t is said that the church is the only institution existing for those who are not its members. This saying is deeply rooted in biblical teaching, which sees the church as the body of Christ that exists to accomplish the Great Commission. The Lord entrusted the church with offering the gospel to the world and building the kingdom of Christ on earth. It is not meant to be a place simply for the service of its members or a club to spend time in until our deaths or the second coming of Christ—whichever occurs first.

However, living up to this church definition will require a change of mentality and direction for most of us. It requires a dynamism of change, updating, and openness. If the church exists for those who are not its members, it must understand what nonmembers need and what mechanisms are appropriate to begin to satisfy those needs.

Most of all, of course, they need salvation and understanding of the purpose of God for their lives. They need teaching, discipleship, and fellowship. There is no dispute about that.

As for the means to satisfy these needs, I believe that each church must conduct a comprehensive field study to see how "non-church members" view these means and what prevents them from attending. In other words, each church needs to know and feel the beat of the street, to realize the tendencies, interests, and what preoccupies the minds and hearts of people. This will help it to determine how to reach the target audience to attract them, draw them closer to it, and offer them the message in an attractive package without compromising the gospel.

If modern and up-to-date music is what will attract them, stop using old hymnody and old musical instruments! The message of the gospel is inspired but music can change. Some hold on to a certain style of music, singing, praise, and liturgy because they are from an old generation and they value heritage, habit, and familiarity. Hymnody and Syriac, Greek, Roman, English, or even incomprehensible classical Arabic words are not inspired. If we find out that these things do not speak to people outside the church, then they have to be changed, or at least modified, to attract them to listen.

Any church tradition that isn't appealing and attractive, or is too far separated from the beat of the streets, should probably be replaced by a style that draws attention and attracts souls. Of course, some would argue that certain music is improper, that perhaps it provokes sin. In any case, each church should examine this matter and find the proper balance.

Our churches are often fixated upon a certain style of praise and singing, and it is difficult for them to accept anything new. Do we accept rap music in church? Do we accept rock and roll? What about classical music? If the answer is "no"—then, what is the reason? Shouldn't we be seeking to attract others after finding out their beat, tendencies, and taste?

This goes beyond mere music and praise to include the preaching of the gospel. Some people are not as patient as Job, and it may be necessary to change terminology, replacing it with a more understandable language that the unchurched person can easily understand.

There is also the matter of quality in presentation. It is simply ridiculous that churches sometimes present programs without good preparation and without entrusting qualified people for each type of work, with a result that lacks in quality. This leads people to get bored and drives them away. They say, "If their message was as important as they claim, they would have invested effort and energy to deliver it with excellence."

Our churches should wake up from dormancy and conduct a good field study on the beat of the street. Ultimately, God moves with the Holy Spirit in our communities—"Apart from me you can do nothing" (John 15:5b)—but he has also asked us to do all we can to help him fulfill the Great Commission of preaching the gospel to all the nations and throughout the earth.

Reflect

What are some ways that the local church can excel in delivering the life-transforming message that Christ has entrusted it with?

John Calvin and personal responsibility in our country

We tend to dislike the word *responsibility*. We love rights, privileges, and benefits, and not so much duties, obligations, or responsibilities.

The concept of responsibility is completely different in the North and West versus the East and South. The US and Canada and other Northern and Western European countries, as well as countries of the Far East, are scientifically developed, economically advanced, and enjoy prosperity, while the Eastern European countries, the Middle East, and countries of Latin America lag and struggle in the same respects. The vast gap between these countries is due to many factors. One of the biggest, I believe, is the impact of the Protestant reform in the sixteenth century.

Five centuries ago, Martin Luther highlighted the concept of personal responsibility in a time when people had buried the concept in the depth of the Bible for ages. Luther stressed the responsibility of each individual to seek salvation, faith, and God's free saving grace.

"The righteous will live by faith," Luther said, from Romans 1:17b. See also Galatians 3:11b and Habakkuk 2:4b for verses that enlightened his heart in this regard. John Calvin—another Protestant reformer who lived in Switzerland and France when Luther was in Germany—introduced the concept from a different angle. Calvin proclaimed that a Christian is called to follow God through his work or profession. This prioritizes the personal responsibility of every human being to work hard in their profession or job. Thus, they demonstrate their faith and bear the fruits of their faith. Calvin goes on to state that working in any profession can be a divine calling, and success in that work can be proof of the blessing and grace of God.

This complements what the Apostle Paul urged us to do when he wrote:

> Whatever you do, work at it with all your heart, as working for the Lord, not for human masters, since you know that you will receive an inheritance from the Lord as a reward. It is the Lord Christ you are serving. (Colossians 3:23–24, see also 3:17)

At the outset of the twentieth century, German sociologist Max Weber attributed the economic progress of North European and American countries to the saturation of Protestant Calvinist thought. This means that their citizens' faith, as taught by their churches, stressed the call of each individual to work actively and distinctively to satisfy God. It is the life of activity and persistence that brought about an unprecedented economic prosperity. This heritage has been preserved and maintained even though the reach of the Protestant church has weakened.

Luther and Calvin collided with the doctrine and practices of the Catholic Church, which called its members to accept the sacraments and to obey the Church. In the Middle East, this teaching collided with the Eastern mentality, which considers that the individual could never be independent or self-reliant but rather must simply be part of a whole. This Eastern mentality cherishes collective, family, and group responsibility. It is a mentality of collaboration and social solidarity in both the positive and negative meanings of these things.

The West embraces individuality and responsibility while the Middle East at least entertains a collective sense of belonging. The individual in the West seems to live to a large extent all by himself and decides all about his life affairs with small influence from the collective. Conversely, Middle Eastern society dictates to individuals what decisions they should make, which values they should adopt, and what things they should or should not do. A simple indication of this is when you meet a person in the West, you'll be asked your name and what you do (your profession), while in the East you will be asked about your family, hometown, and background. It's easy to spot our different way of thinking.

Of course, I do not mean that we in the East should abandon social solidarity and family relations, but these should be put in their proper context so that they don't overwhelm all aspects of life and cause the elimination of personal responsibility.

The thinking that celebrates personal responsibility has led recruitment in developed countries to be based on competencies, while in communities that lack that thinking, recruitment is based on mediations and favors. For the former countries, this thinking has led to the identification of measurable goals, while in the latter countries, it has led to random courses of action without clear goals. This thinking has led to accurate accountability and benchmark systems for each employee in developed countries, while it has led to the lack of accountability and benchmarks where that thinking is absent.

The adoption of John Calvin's teaching is necessary both on the church level and on the individual level. We need to adopt the highest degree of personal responsibility and benchmarks in Christ's service. The call of Christ, which we aim to follow as his disciples, relies upon individual responsibility of working diligently, faithfully, and distinctly, and is indispensable for every believer.

Reflect

How does your country balance personal responsibility and social solidarity with the weak? Is this balance desirable, and why?

Will the Eastern Church survive the European fate?

Whoever is following global changes can witness the decline of Christianity in Europe to the extent that it is not considered a Christian continent anymore! *The Guardian* newspaper in London reports that the percentage of citizens who identify as "religious" today is very low, and those that attend church on Sundays are also very few. Hence, the influence of the church has turned out to be marginal.

No one can deny that European countries were established on Christian values and foundations. However, when the citizens of those countries were given the freedom to choose, the great majority, unfortunately, expressed themselves by saying they do not care about Christianity or what the church has to offer. They began to stop attending church services decades or centuries ago.

Is there a threat that the Middle Eastern church's fate might be similar to what has happened in Europe?

The answer to this question is complex, because the history of our countries, their evolution, and the dynamism of life in them is different from what Europe has gone through. In the last century, Europe was involved heavily in the two world wars. Europe then witnessed the spread of many philosophies and trends, and it experienced a diversity of ethnicities and sects that were in conflict with one another. Some European countries reached an unprecedented economic boom.

The identity of an Arab Christian in Israel is bound by his or her denomination because of the Eastern context and due to the fact that Christians constitute a numerically minuscule minority. This may contribute to the church's maintenance of its central role or at least delays its decay. On the other hand, globalization and easy communication may suggest otherwise. Equally pessimistic, the prevailing intellectual currents here in Israel and the general way of life that mimics European attitudes and trends suggest that the fate of the church may be on a similar path. Philosophical and intellectual currents that spread like wildfire in Europe are now present in our country through university education. The theories of evolution, relativity, scientific criticism, and streams of nationalism, agnosticism, some forms of feminism, atheism, and others have found an unchecked idealistic incubator here, especially among the educated, whose percentage of the population is increasingly growing.

But the issue is not only the intellectual currents that are growing and spreading, but also our approaches for dealing with them. If church leaders want to address these currents to ward off their dangers, we need a Christian approach that seeks to convince the mind and does not avoid the difficult questions that are being raised.

An additional challenge is the penetration of electronic means of communication, especially smartphones. These have placed the whole world in the palm of our hand, causing competition with the church to become very intense indeed. Because of this, the local preacher of today has to compete for attention with the world's best preachers, who broadcast their sermons. The leader of praise and worship in the church who is usually accompanied by one musical instrument has to compete with talented worship leaders armed with high-level musical choirs. Church members have replaced their face-to-face mutual relationships with virtual relationships on social networking sites behind their smartphone's screen.

Does the church have any hope of winning this competition at a time when it is still stuck with its archaic mechanisms and methods? It has not yet realized that the worn-out steam-powered train has been replaced by a sophisticated cellular one that has already left the station. In order to be considered relevant today, I believe we must:

1. Equip ministers and leaders with tools to study the Word of God with an understanding of contemporary philosophies from a Christian perspective.
2- Establish a vision for communicating the message of the gospel in creative and new ways, to bring hope and enkindle excitement in people's hearts.
3. Keep pace with modernity and progress fearlessly. We should make use of our professional people to adopt and utilize new innovative mechanisms to reach the lost in twenty-first-century ways.
4. Put away flattery, falsehood, hypocrisy, and fake relationships. True relationships and selfless love appeal to those who believe the church is not relevant in their lives.
5. Be obedient to the Lord's command to love God and to love our neighbors as ourselves; this should be translated into practical action for the sake of justice, restoring the oppressed and helping the poor.

When the church stands up faithfully and intelligently, it earns respect and appreciation, and the world listens to what it has to say. Will those of us in Eastern countries do these things, rising and renewing ourselves, avoiding the phantom of weakness and aging that felled the church in Europe?

Reflect

What safeguards can be put in place today to prevent a dim fate for the church in your country?

A calling to be an Arab

God has created me as an Arab. I sometimes wish he had created me differently.

Arab people, Muslims and Christians alike, are simple, hospitable, and generous people. Unfortunately, and at this stage in history, they are characterized among the nations as backward people immersed in violence, radicalism, oppression, and dictatorship.

A person cannot change his skin, or a leopard its spots, and likewise it will not help the Arab if he speaks a foreign language without an accent, if he wears a tuxedo, or replaces his black eyes with blue contact lenses. In his chest, there will always be a pulsating Arab heart.

Fall has taken what was once a hopeful Arab spring by surprise, causing it to darken and turn the color of its leaves to yellow. Soon, those leaves will fly away, if they haven't already, scattering our dreams and uncovering our flaws. This atrocious time comes with a darker cloud over Christian Arabs than over anyone else in the Middle East.

Christian Arabs are ridiculed because they are few, but their answer is, "Few will find the narrow gate." The temptation for them to emigrate is great, as the West enjoys peace, equality, and respect for all human beings regardless of color and race. The West is like a magnet that attracts Arab Christians who are fed up with the way things are. A university degree is their passport, and a Green Card is like fresh fruit that's waiting for its picker.

The legions of evil and the demons that came from the pit of hell were waiting at the cross of Golgotha, counting the remaining number of Jesus's groans, expecting his death. They danced joyfully when he breathed his last. Jesus confronted them, uprooted them, and spoiled their dissolute party when he rose victoriously. Shall we flee from his own country while our Lord is the Lion of the tribe of Judah who has prevailed?

He chose us to be witnesses among our Arab people. He does not leave himself without witness in every nation, tongue, and people. He does not want *a witness who has seen nothing* (the title of a famous, comical, Egyptian play) but a witness who speaks boldly with truthful testimony. He wants a witness who has been satisfied by the Lord's honey.

We pray to God that there will never be a day when Christ's land turns into a land of Arab Christian graves and stone. May it always be a land of living Christian witnesses whose lives speak about the holy and righteous God.

God created Arabs in his image and likeness and did not exclude them when he said, "For God so loved the world . . ." His love has knocked on the door of every sinner, calling each one of us by name. Similarly, our love must knock at the door of Khaled, Ahmad, Farid, Majed, Ali, and Anton in every street, alley, and neighborhood all around the Arab world in Minya, Benghazi, Salt, Lattakia, Doha, Mosul, Deir Hanna, and Halhul. This love is not general and abstract but concrete and specific; many waters of hatred cannot quench love.

God's thoughts are higher than our thoughts and so are his ways from our ways, and so God created us as Arabs. Therefore, we will not say: "If it is possible, let this cup pass from me," but rather: "Not my will, but yours, be done."

Reflect

1. Do you suffer also from your ethnicity? What do you do to overcome it?
2. Mention two examples from the Bible of people who cared about the welfare of their people.

ACKNOWLEDGMENTS

I pray that my stand on a cliff of the Precipice is not a stand in an ivory tower, but a position ingrained in the daily life of the people in each of my sub-identities, and certainly under the lordship of Christ.

Thanks to Ragaa Ezat for her excellent translation of the articles, to Manda Van Kalsbeek for her edits and insights, to Mike Brookshire and Lamma Mansour for their review and comments, and to the Rev. Dr. Jeff Moes and the Sunnybrook Family for their support, and Bana Haddad for the work of design.

Above all, I thank the Lord for his favor and for enabling me to contribute to the Christian library worldwide from my unique setting.

ABOUT THE AUTHOR

Botrus Mansour was born in Nazareth in 1965. As a child he lived in Jerusalem, Oxford, and Nazareth. After he graduated from Nazareth Baptist School, Botrus completed a law degree at the Hebrew University in Jerusalem (1991), was admitted to the Israeli Bar Association (1993), and practiced Law in Haifa and Nazareth. In 2004 he was invited to lead Nazareth Baptist School as the General Director, a position he still holds. In 2009 Botrus completed an MBA from Haifa University and later completed a teaching certificate in Civics from the Open University (2018).

Botrus has been active in leadership positions in church and parachurch organizations and has held various positions including Chairman of The Convention of Evangelical Churches in Israel, Secretary of the Alliance of Evangelical Conventions in Jordan and the Holy land, Vice Chairman of the Association of Baptist Churches in Israel, member of the Executive Committee for Christian Schools in Israel, Deputy Chairman of "Nazareth Village" board, Member of Global Council of Advocates International, Co-Chairman of the Lausanne Initiative for Reconciliation Israel-Palestine, Chairman of Students committee in the Fellowship of Christian Students in Israel, Board member of Musalaha, Founding member and elder in the Local Baptist Church—Nazareth, co-chair of and contributor to the trilingual web site *comeandsee.com*, Co-Founder of Cana Wedding Chapel in Cana of Galilee, and others.

Botrus has also been involved in giving lectures in churches, universities, and conferences in Israel, the USA, Canada, different European countries, Jordan, Egypt, and Taiwan on matters of faith and life in the Middle East. He has also written extensively in Arabic, Hebrew, and English and has published in *Christianity Today*, *Haaretz*, and other media, as well as publishing several books, including *When Your Neighbor is the Savior* (Hope Publishing house, 2011).

Botrus and his wife, A'bir, have two grown children and a teenager. They live in Nazareth.

To contact him:

Botrus Mansour

P.O. Box 1, Nazareth 1610001, Israel

Email: botrusm@gmail.com

+972-52-5322060

ABOUT PARACLETE PRESS

Who We Are

As the publishing arm of the Community of Jesus, Paraclete Press presents a full expression of Christian belief and practice—from Catholic to Evangelical, from Protestant to Orthodox, reflecting the ecumenical charism of the Community and its dedication to sacred music, the fine arts, and the written word. We publish books, recordings, sheet music, and video/DVDs that nourish the vibrant life of the church and its people.

What We Are Doing

BOOKS | PARACLETE PRESS BOOKS show the richness and depth of what it means to be Christian. While Benedictine spirituality is at the heart of who we are and all that we do, our books reflect the Christian experience across many cultures, time periods, and houses of worship.

We have many series, including *Paraclete Essentials*; *Paraclete Fiction*; *Paraclete Poetry*; *Paraclete Giants*; and for children and adults, *All God's Creatures*, books about animals and faith; and *San Damiano Books*, focusing on Franciscan spirituality. Others include *Voices from the Monastery* (men and women monastics writing about living a spiritual life today), *Active Prayer*, and new for young readers: *The Pope's Cat*. We also specialize in gift books for children on the occasions of Baptism and First Communion, as well as other important times in a child's life, and books that bring creativity and liveliness to any adult spiritual life.

The MOUNT TABOR BOOKS series focuses on the arts and literature as well as liturgical worship and spirituality; it was created in conjunction with the Mount Tabor Ecumenical Centre for Art and Spirituality in Barga, Italy.

MUSIC | PARACLETE PRESS DISTRIBUTES RECORDINGS of the internationally acclaimed choir *Gloriæ Dei Cantores*, the *Gloriæ Dei Cantores Schola*, and the other instrumental artists of the *Arts Empowering Life Foundation*.

PARACLETE PRESS IS THE EXCLUSIVE NORTH AMERICAN DISTRIBUTOR for the Gregorian chant recordings from St. Peter's Abbey in Solesmes, France. Paraclete also carries all of the Solesmes chant publications for Mass and the Divine Office, as well as their academic research publications.

In addition, PARACLETE PRESS SHEET MUSIC publishes the work of today's finest composers of sacred choral music, annually reviewing over 1,000 works and releasing between 40 and 60 works for both choir and organ.

VIDEO | Our video/DVDs offer spiritual help, healing, and biblical guidance for a broad range of life issues including grief and loss, marriage, forgiveness, facing death, understanding suicide, bullying, addictions, Alzheimer's, and Christian formation.

Learn more about us at our website:
www.paracletepress.com
or phone us toll-free at 1.800.451.5006

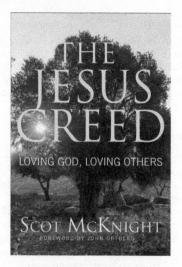